AIRCRAFT
A/R/C/H/I/V/E
BOMBERS OF WORLD WAR TWO

Argus Books Limited
Wolsey House
Wolsey Road
Hemel Hempstead
Herts. HP2 4SS
England

First published by Argus Books 1988

© In this Collection Argus Books 1988

ISBN 0 85242 968 1

Designed by Little Oak Studios
Phototypesetting by Typesetters (Birmingham) Ltd
Printed and bound in Great Britain at the University Printing House,
Oxford

Cover photo: Charles E. Brown (R.A.F. Museum Collection)

Contents

A DETAILED COLLECTION OF ORIGINAL SCALE AIRCRAFT DRAWINGS

Introduction

Ever since the early pioneers exercised a satanic streak in their personalities by dropping assorted ironmongery from fragile cockpits on to unfortunate infantry, the bomber has occupied military strategists in a constant search for improved forms of wilful destruction. This was never more evident than in the years 1939–45, the period which this volume covers, from the plodding Fairey Battle over France and the Do 17 and He 111 Luftwaffe mainstays to the Privateer and Arado Blitz which came just too late to displace effectively the Fortress, Liberator, Lancaster and Halifax as the real workhorses of World War II.

Bombers can range from the incredibly adaptable Swordfish, the fearsome Ju 87 Stuka and the heroic Ilyushin Stormovik to the slippery Martin Marauder. Each has had its main purpose, in some cases far removed from the original intention; but for the enthusiastic plane watcher, the bomber represents an aeroplane apart from all others – designed to dispose of enormous weights far from home base and with an essential precision that demands special training and discipline.

The mixture in these papers embraces these classic types in approximate chronological order so that the pattern of design progress – and tactical demands – becomes evident as the pages are turned. Producing these drawings of larger aeroplanes has its own problems: measuring a high-level wing, or a very long sloping fuselage, is an obvious hazard, but less apparent are the odd variations introduced by, for example a change of engine or defensive armament. The hours of study behind the drawings is all too easily overlooked.

Each drawing is a typical example of the skill and dedication applied by an amateur researcher after measurement and photographic interpretation to produce something which, in fact, very few manufacturers are able to provide! For it may come as a surprise, but the reality is that the manufacturer's general arrangement drawings have little value in the factories, are rarely accurate in shape or scale and, without exception, illustrate the aeroplane in a stage long since superseded by production variants.

Access to the real thing is the ideal, but how can one measure each panel, check every angle and record all the shapes? It takes a special sort of dedication to undertake such a mammoth task – a museum visit will confirm the enormity of the undertaking.

Demand for accuracy and authenticity originated through the work of James Hay Stevens in 'Aeromodeller'. He was among the first to adopt 1/72nd scale, based on the Imperial measure of one sixth of an inch representing one foot. Opening standards, as set by James Stevens, were taken up through the series of *Aircraft of the Fighting Powers* volumes published by Harborough, once an associated company with MAP. Wartime urgency quickly generated a new breed of detail draughtsman, typified by Harry Cooper and Owen Thetford. After seven volumes and the creation of an *Aircraft Described* series in 'Aeromodeller' centred on civil

The Fairey Battle light bomber, which suffered grievously in the early part of the war. Plans appear on pages 10–15.
▼

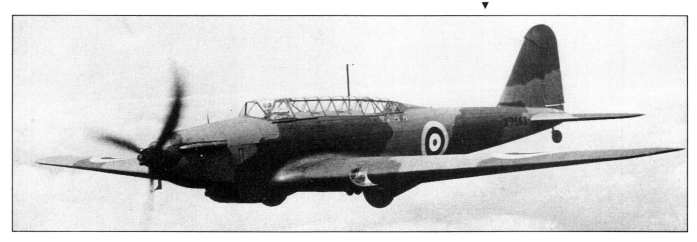

◄ A draughtsman's dream – but photos like this one, showing a true plan view of a B-17, are rare indeed.

aircraft by Eddie Riding, 1/72nd scale was firmly established, and the fine detail in the drawings reached levels of intricacy to satisy the most demanding enthusiast. As aeroplanes became larger, so the reduced scales of 1/144th and 1/96th were introduced to contain the drawings within magazine pages. So it is the same in these pages; readers seeking larger prints of the same drawings can obtain them from the Plans Service as advertised on page 96.

From the immediate postwar years to the present day, the levels of minutiae have soared far beyond the first conceptions. Out of *Aircraft Described* came *Aeroplanes in Outline* and *Famous Biplanes* and, through years of publication in 'Aeromodeller' magazine, a band of skilled contributors built up a series which now comes in book form.

The drawings reflect the individual character of the originator. Each was in its time a labour of love, the fruits of which have been the immense pleasure given to students, collectors and aeromodellers. If by reproduction in this form we commemorate their work permanently, rather than in a transient monthly magazine, then we will have rewarded both the draughtsmen and the reader with a treasure store.

Fairey Swordfish Mks I and II

Country of origin: Great Britain.
Type: Two- or three-seat, carrier-based torpedo-bomber/spotter/reconnaissance aircraft.
Dimensions: Wing span 45ft 6in *13.87m*; length 35ft 8in *10.87m*; height 12ft 4in *3.76m*; wing area 607 sq ft *56.39m²*.
Weights: Empty 4700lb *2132kg*; loaded (torpedo-bomber) 7510lb *2289kg*,

(reconnaissance configuration) 6750lb *3061kg*.
Powerplant: One Bristol Pegasus 30 nine-cylinder radial engine rated at 750hp.
Performance: Maximum speed 144mph *232kph* at 5000ft *1525m*; time to 10,000ft *3050m*, 10min; service ceiling 10,500ft *3200m*; range (clean) 770 miles *1240km*.

Armament: Torpedo, mine or bombs up to 1500lb *680kg*, (Mk II, optional) eight 60lb *27kg* or 25lb *11.3kg* rocket projectiles; one fixed and one flexibly mounted 0.303in machine gun.
Service: First flight (TSR I) 21 March 1933, (TSR II) 17 April 1934; service entry (Mk I) July 1936.

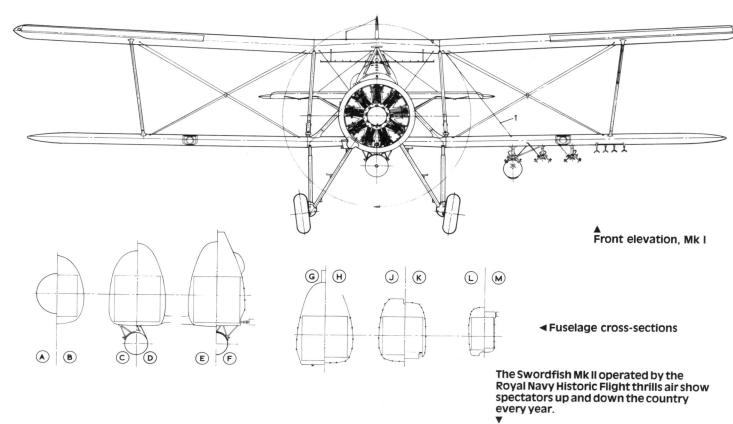

▲ Front elevation, Mk I

◄ Fuselage cross-sections

The Swordfish Mk II operated by the Royal Navy Historic Flight thrills air show spectators up and down the country every year.
▼

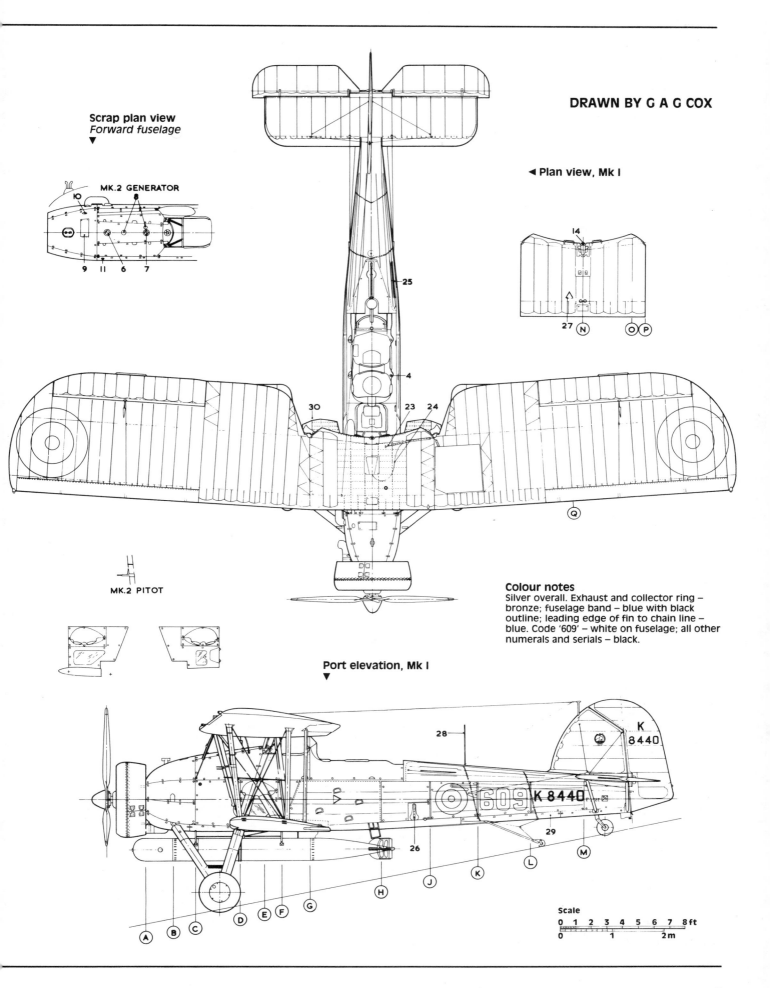

Scrap plan view
Forward fuselage
▼

MK.2 GENERATOR

MK.2 PITOT

DRAWN BY G A G COX

◄ Plan view, Mk I

Colour notes
Silver overall. Exhaust and collector ring – bronze; fuselage band – blue with black outline; leading edge of fin to chain line – blue. Code '609' – white on fuselage; all other numerals and serials – black.

Port elevation, Mk I
▼

K 8440

609 K 8440

Scale
0 1 2 3 4 5 6 7 8 ft
0   1   2 m

Front elevation, Mk II
Wings in folded position
▼

Wing cross-sections
▼

MK.2 OIL
COOLER

Underplan, Mk I
Wings in folded position
▲

Numerical key

1. Extra wire to leading edge when bombs are carried in wing racks. **2.** Torpedo sight bars. Miniature lamps are equally spaced along upper edges. Electric cables are cleated to front centre-section struts. **3.** Hoisting sling of 100cwt cable attached to upper longerons at base of rear centre-section struts. Free ends of cables are stowed in box in upper centre-section with 45cwt stay cables which attach to front spar on aircraft centreline. **4.** Mountings for Type 0-3 compass. Note asymmetric layout. **5.** Part of larger, 20-element oil cooler blanked off by small aluminium plate. **6.** Petrol filler cap, main tank. **7.** Petrol filler cap, gravity tank. **8.** Petrol gauges. **9.** Access to oil filler cap. **10.** Oil tank immersion heater. **11.** Inertia starter socket. **12.** This step should be removed when machine is fitted with floats. **13.** Handling rail fitted in place of tailwheel on seaplane. **14.** Aileron wires run parallel to rear centre-section struts to rocking head assembly which is connected to ailerons by push-pull tubes. Rotating handwheel imparts downward bias to ailerons of 8° so that they act as flaps for catapult take-off. **15.** Metal covering to undersides as far out as here on Mk II and Mk III. **16.** Forward synchronised gun rarely fitted. **17.** Wing locking handles. **18.** Bomb-aimer's retracting windshield. **19.** Bomb-aimer's sliding hatch. Camera sometimes fitted above. **20.** Seaplane towing bridle. Cable is spring-clipped to lower and then upper ends of inner front float struts. **21.** Catapult spools. **22.** Metal step plate over balsa fairings. **23.** Dinghy release cord. Small handle was provided on upper centre-section for pilot; another cable ran down rear centre-section strut and along outside of fuselage on starboard side level with upper longeron as far as tailplane. **24.** Cable from dinghy in port upper wing to immersion switch on firewall. Dinghy was automatically inflated if aircraft was submerged. **25.** Zip access to sea anchor. **26.** Narrow window disclosing six lead ballast weights mounted on lower longeron on each side of aircraft. **27.** Zip inspection flaps. **28.** Rod aerial fitted to all but early models. **29.** Fairing panel around arrester hook 'A' frame. Note that groove for frame is wider on port side to accommodate the hydraulic damper. This panel was replaced by another without grooves when hook was removed for seaplane operations. **30.** Limit of metal and anti-skid covering to lower stub plane. **31.** Red warning bands on floats. **32.** Wings are shown rotated about their rear spars in this view to show full chord. .

Note: K8440 was an 822 Squadron machine aboard HMS *Courageous*, and is shown in drawing in its 1939 colouring. There is no evidence that this particular machine was ever fitted with floats. Modellers wishing to build the seaplane version are advised to substitute L2742 for K8440, and 529 for 609, or to model the prototype K4190; both these machines have been photographed fitted with floats.

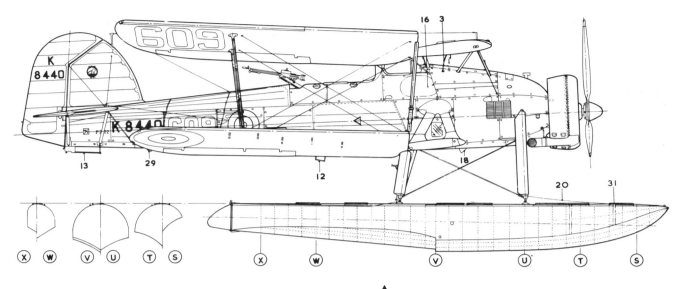

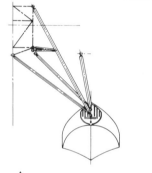

▲
Float cross-sections

▲
Starboard elevation, Mk I floatplane
Wings in folded position

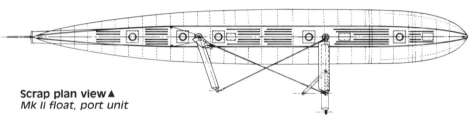

Scrap plan view▲
Mk II float, port unit

▲
Scrap front elevation
Mk II float, port unit

Salutes from the crew as the RN's preserved Swordfish shows its paces. Despite its apparent obsolescence, the aircraft performed legendary feats during World War II.
▼

Fairey Battle B Mk I

Country of origin: Great Britain.
Type: Two-seat, land-based light bomber.
Dimensions: Wing span 54ft 0in *16.46m*; length 52ft 1¾in *15.89m*; height 15ft 6in *4.72m*; wing area 422 sq ft *39.2m²*.
Weights: Empty 6647lb *3015kg*; loaded 10,792lb *4894kg*.

Powerplant: One Rolls-Royce Merlin I V12, liquid-cooled piston engine rated at 1036hp.
Performance: Maximum speed 257mph *414kph* at 15,000ft *4570m*; time to 10,000ft *3050m*, 8.4min; service ceiling 25,000ft *7620m*; range 640 miles *1030km*.
Armament: Up to 1000lb *454kg* of bombs

in wing bays and 500lb *227kg* on external racks, plus one fixed and one flexibly mounted 0.303in Browning machine gun.
Service: First flight (prototype) 10 March 1936; service entry 20 March 1937.

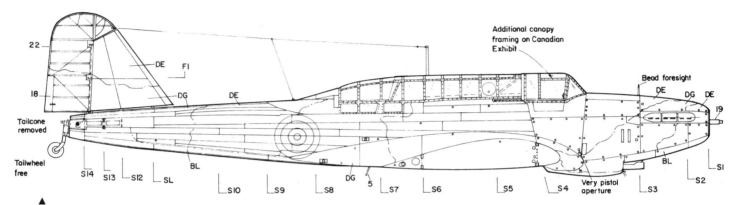

▲
Starboard elevation
Wing omitted to show detail

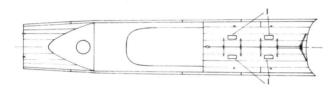

Scrap views
Fairing panel and canopy removed to show structure of rear cockpit
◄▼

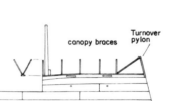

Canadian Air Force Battle B Mk I in standard camouflage.
▼

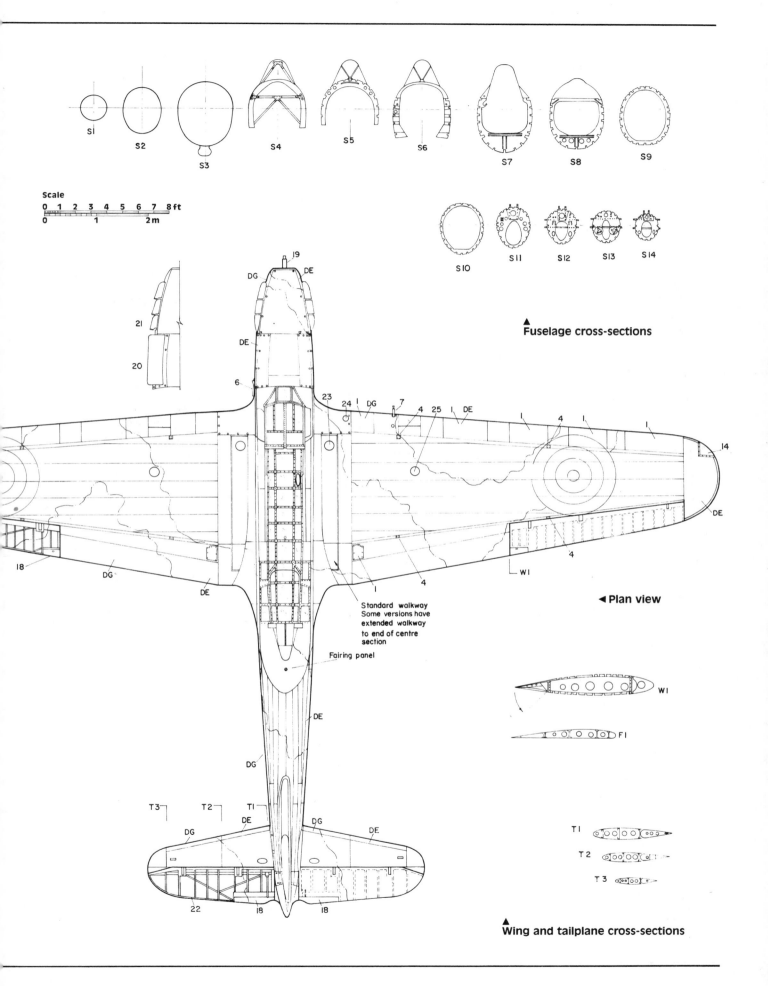

Scale

0 1 2 3 4 5 6 7 8 ft
0 1 2 m

S1 S2 S3 S4 S5 S6 S7 S8 S9

S10 S11 S12 S13 S14

▲ Fuselage cross-sections

Standard walkway
Some versions have
extended walkway
to end of centre
section

Fairing panel

◄ Plan view

W1

F1

T1
T2
T3

▲ Wing and tailplane cross-sections

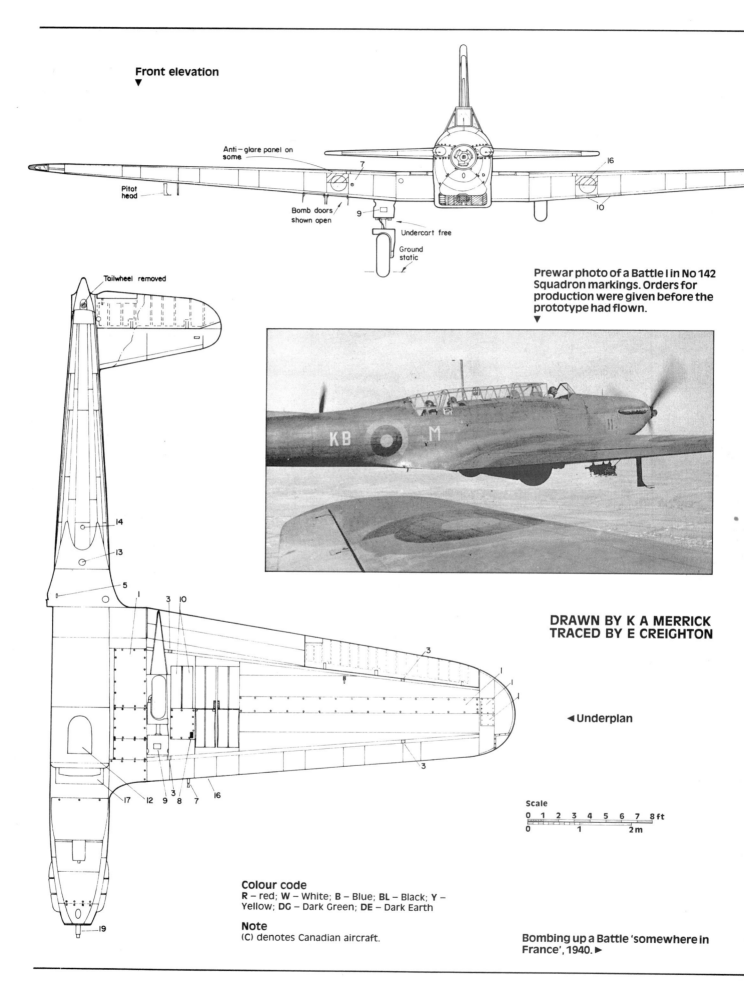

Front elevation
▼

Anti-glare panel on some.

Pitot head

Bomb doors shown open

7

9

Undercart free

Ground static

16

10

Tailwheel removed

14

13

5

1

3 10

3

3

17 12 9 8 7 16

19

Prewar photo of a Battle I in No 142 Squadron markings. Orders for production were given before the prototype had flown.
▼

DRAWN BY K A MERRICK
TRACED BY E CREIGHTON

◄ Underplan

Scale
0 1 2 3 4 5 6 7 8 ft
0 1 2 m

Colour code
R – red; **W** – White; **B** – Blue; **BL** – Black; **Y** – Yellow; **DG** – Dark Green; **DE** – Dark Earth

Note
(C) denotes Canadian aircraft.

Bombing up a Battle 'somewhere in France', 1940. ►

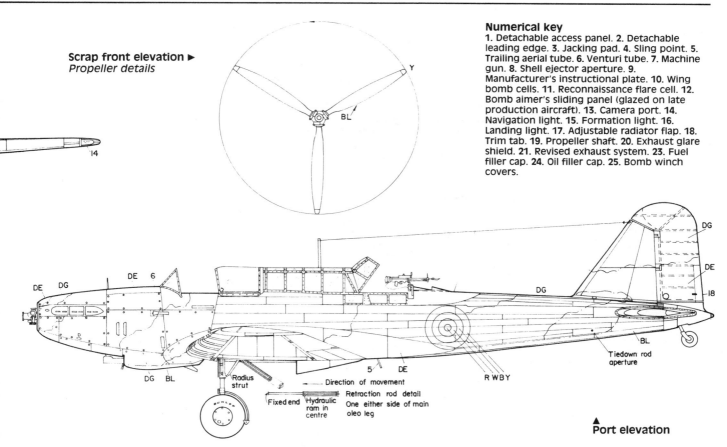

Scrap front elevation ▶
Propeller details

Numerical key
1. Detachable access panel. 2. Detachable leading edge. 3. Jacking pad. 4. Sling point. 5. Trailing aerial tube. 6. Venturi tube. 7. Machine gun. 8. Shell ejector aperture. 9. Manufacturer's instructional plate. 10. Wing bomb cells. 11. Reconnaissance flare cell. 12. Bomb aimer's sliding panel (glazed on late production aircraft). 13. Camera port. 14. Navigation light. 15. Formation light. 16. Landing light. 17. Adjustable radiator flap. 18. Trim tab. 19. Propeller shaft. 20. Exhaust glare shield. 21. Revised exhaust system. 23. Fuel filler cap. 24. Oil filler cap. 25. Bomb winch covers.

Radius strut

Fixed end
Hydraulic ram in centre

Direction of movement
Retraction rod detail
One either side of main oleo leg

Tiedown rod aperture

▲ **Port elevation**

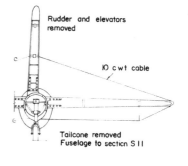

Rudder and elevators removed

10 cwt cable

Tailcone removed
Fuselage to section S 11

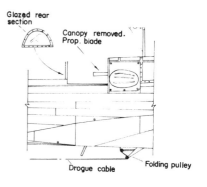

Glazed rear section

Canopy removed. Prop. blade

Drogue cable

Folding pulley

▶ Routine maintenance in the field. Note the shrouded exhausts.

◀ N2042 was converted to take a Bristol Hercules radial engine.

Port elevation and scrap views
Two-seat trainer
▼

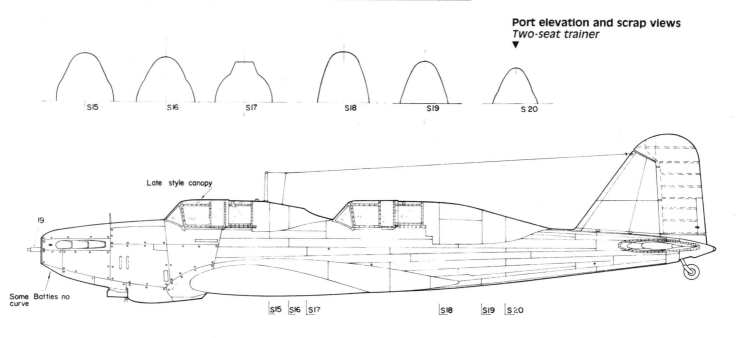

S15   S16   S17   S18   S19   S 20

Late style canopy

19

Some Battles no curve

S15 S16 S17   S18   S19 S 20

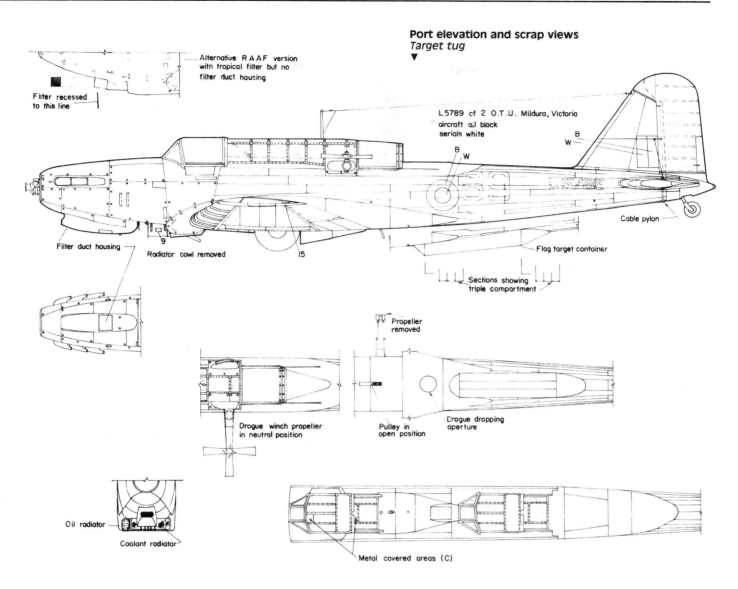

Port elevation and scrap views
Target tug
▼

Filter recessed
to this line

Alternative R A A F version
with tropical filter but no
filter duct housing

L5789 of 2 O.T.U. Mildura, Victoria
aircraft all black
serials white

B
W

W ── B

B
W

Cable pylon

Filter duct housing

Radiator cowl removed

9

15

Flag target container

Sections showing
triple compartment

Propeller
removed

Drogue winch propeller
in neutral position

Pulley in
open position

Drogue dropping
aperture

Oil radiator

Coolant radiator

Metal covered areas (C)

The RAAF also operated Battles, principally TT.I target tugs, as here.
▼

V1201

Junkers Ju 86A, D and E

Country of origin: Germany.
Type: Land-based medium bomber.
Dimensions: (D) Wing span 73ft 9¾in *22.50m*; length 58ft 7½in *17.87m*; height 16ft 7¼in *5.06m*; wing area 882.65 sq ft *82.0m²*.
Weights: (D) Empty 11,356lb *5150kg*; empty equipped 11,797lb *5350kg*; loaded 17,772lb *8060kg*; maximum 18,081lb *8200kg*.
Powerplant: (D) Two Junkers Jumo 205C-4 piston engines each rated at 600hp.
Performance: (D) Maximum speed 202mph *325kph* at 9850ft *3000m*; service ceiling 19,360ft *5900m*; range 932 miles *1500km*.
Armament: Up to 1765lb *800kg* of bombs in fuselage cells; three flexibly mounted 7.9mm MG 15 machine guns.
Service: First flight (Ju 86ab1) 4 November 1934; service entry (A) spring 1936, (D) early 1937, (E) summer 1937.

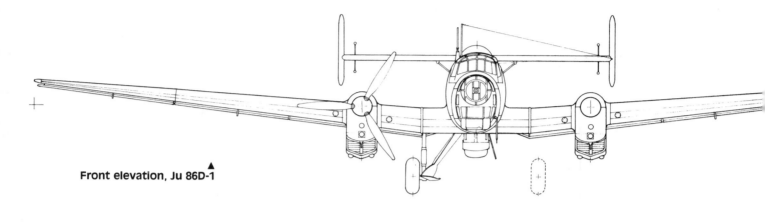

▲ Front elevation, Ju 86D-1

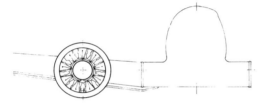
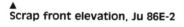

▲ Scrap front elevation, Ju 86E-2

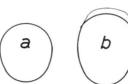 a b 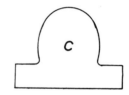 c d

▲ Fuselage cross-sections

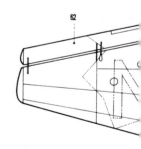

Scale
0 1 2 3 4 5 6 7 8 ft
0 1 2m

◀ Ju 86D-1s in Luftwaffe service. The aircraft first fought in the Spanish Civil War.

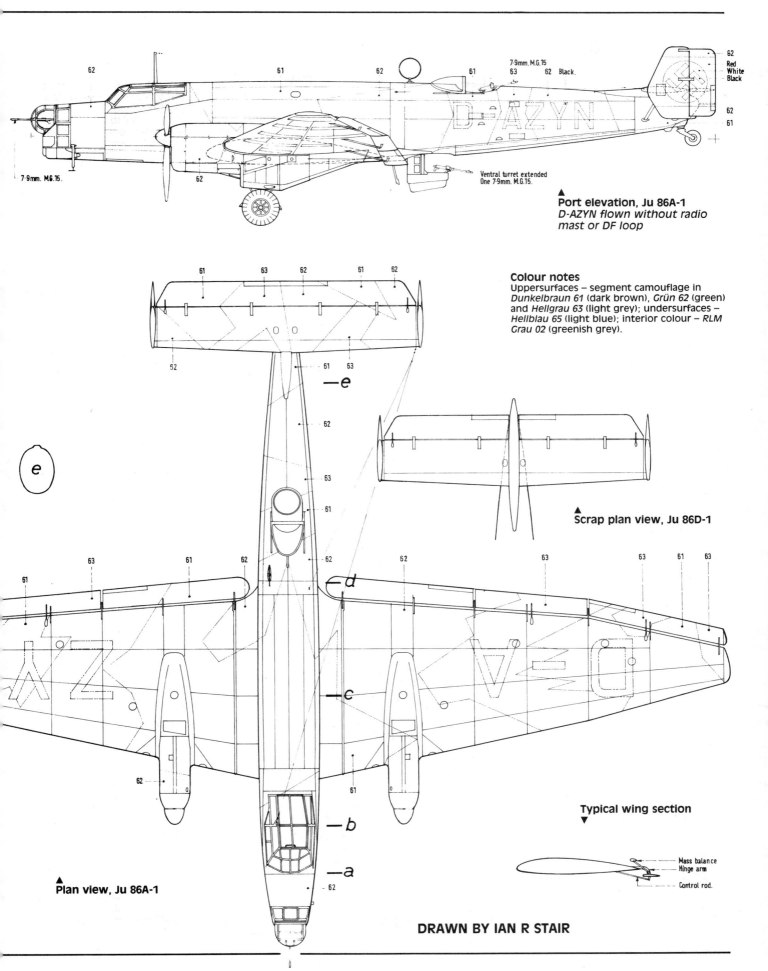

62

62

61

7·9mm. M.G.15

61

62

63 62 Black.

62
Red
White
Black

62
61

7·9mm. M.G.15.

62

Ventral turret extended
One 7·9mm. M.G.15.

▲ **Port elevation, Ju 86A-1**
*D-AZYN flown without radio
mast or DF loop*

61 63 62 61 62

Colour notes
Uppersurfaces – segment camouflage in
Dunkelbraun 61 (dark brown), *Grün 62* (green)
and *Hellgrau 63* (light grey); undersurfaces –
Hellblau 65 (light blue); interior colour – *RLM
Grau 02* (greenish grey).

62

61 63

—*e*

e

62

63

61

62

▲ **Scrap plan view, Ju 86D-1**

63 61 62 62 62 63 63 61 63

61

—*d*

—*c*

62

61

Typical wing section
▼

—*b*

—*a*

62

▲ **Plan view, Ju 86A-1**

Mass balance
Hinge arm

Control rod.

DRAWN BY IAN R STAIR

17

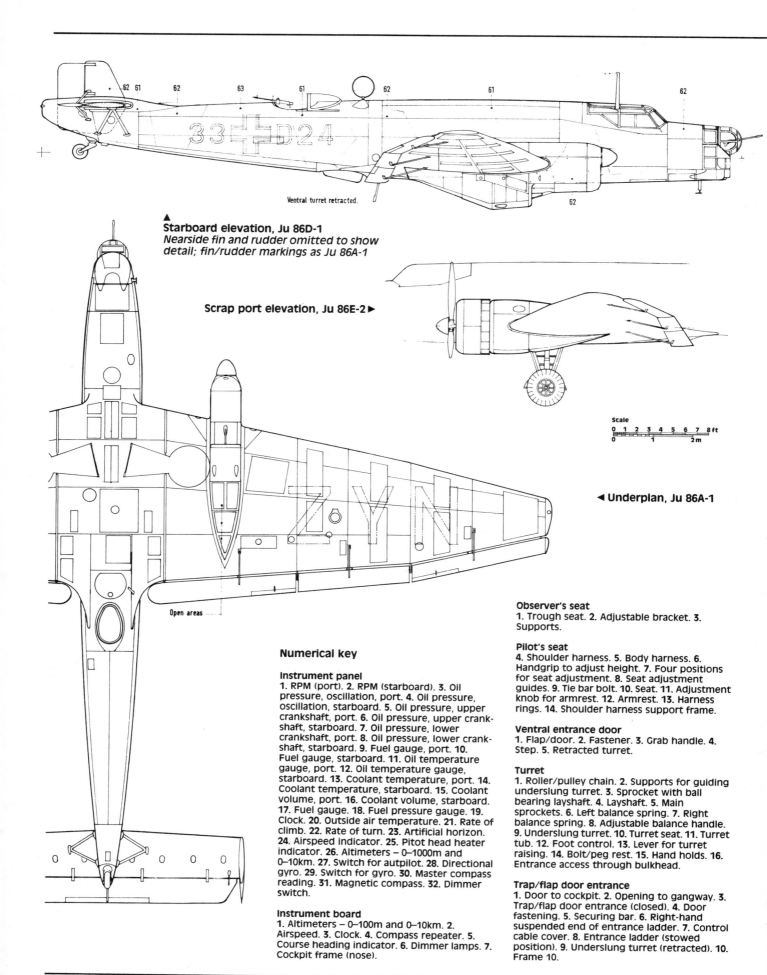

Starboard elevation, Ju 86D-1
Nearside fin and rudder omitted to show detail; fin/rudder markings as Ju 86A-1

Ventral turret retracted.

Scrap port elevation, Ju 86E-2 ►

◄ **Underplan, Ju 86A-1**

Open areas

Scale
0 1 2 3 4 5 6 7 8 ft
0 1 2m

Numerical key

Instrument panel
1. RPM (port). 2. RPM (starboard). 3. Oil pressure, oscillation, port. 4. Oil pressure, oscillation, starboard. 5. Oil pressure, upper crankshaft, port. 6. Oil pressure, upper crankshaft, starboard. 7. Oil pressure, lower crankshaft, port. 8. Oil pressure, lower crankshaft, starboard. 9. Fuel gauge, port. 10. Fuel gauge, starboard. 11. Oil temperature gauge, port. 12. Oil temperature gauge, starboard. 13. Coolant temperature, port. 14. Coolant temperature, starboard. 15. Coolant volume, port. 16. Coolant volume, starboard. 17. Fuel gauge. 18. Fuel pressure gauge. 19. Clock. 20. Outside air temperature. 21. Rate of climb. 22. Rate of turn. 23. Artificial horizon. 24. Airspeed indicator. 25. Pitot head heater indicator. 26. Altimeters – 0–1000m and 0–10km. 27. Switch for autpilot. 28. Directional gyro. 29. Switch for gyro. 30. Master compass reading. 31. Magnetic compass. 32. Dimmer switch.

Instrument board
1. Altimeters – 0–100m and 0–10km. 2. Airspeed. 3. Clock. 4. Compass repeater. 5. Course heading indicator. 6. Dimmer lamps. 7. Cockpit frame (nose).

Observer's seat
1. Trough seat. 2. Adjustable bracket. 3. Supports.

Pilot's seat
4. Shoulder harness. 5. Body harness. 6. Handgrip to adjust height. 7. Four positions for seat adjustment. 8. Seat adjustment guides. 9. Tie bar bolt. 10. Seat. 11. Adjustment knob for armrest. 12. Armrest. 13. Harness rings. 14. Shoulder harness support frame.

Ventral entrance door
1. Flap/door. 2. Fastener. 3. Grab handle. 4. Step. 5. Retracted turret.

Turret
1. Roller/pulley chain. 2. Supports for guiding underslung turret. 3. Sprocket with ball bearing layshaft. 4. Layshaft. 5. Main sprockets. 6. Left balance spring. 7. Right balance spring. 8. Adjustable balance handle. 9. Underslung turret. 10. Turret seat. 11. Turret tub. 12. Foot control. 13. Lever for turret raising. 14. Bolt/peg rest. 15. Hand holds. 16. Entrance access through bulkhead.

Trap/flap door entrance
1. Door to cockpit. 2. Opening to gangway. 3. Trap/flap door entrance (closed). 4. Door fastening. 5. Securing bar. 6. Right-hand suspended end of entrance ladder. 7. Control cable cover. 8. Entrance ladder (stowed position). 9. Underslung turret (retracted). 10. Frame 10.

Scrap view ▼
Instrument panel

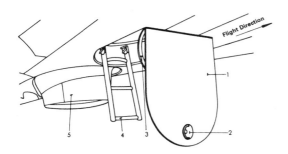

Scrap view
Ventral entrance door

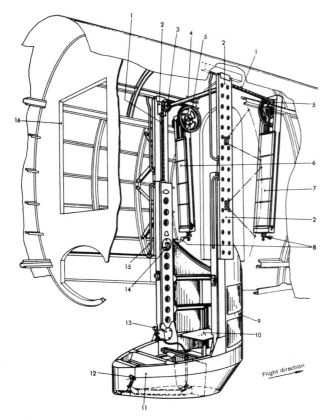

Flight direction

▲
Scrap view
Underslung turret (extended)

Scrap view
Instrument board (observer)
▼

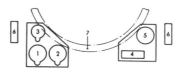

Scrap view ▶
Adjustable seat (observer)

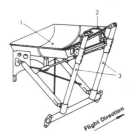

Flight Direction

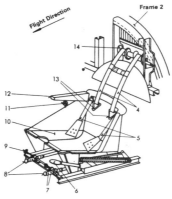

Flight Direction

Frame 2

◀ **Scrap view**
Adjustable seat (pilot)

Scrap view
Trap/flap door entrance and underslung turret (facing cockpit)
▼

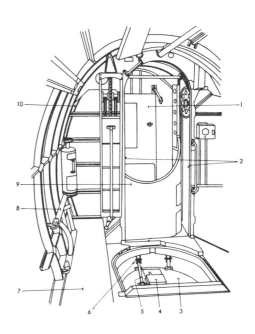

Dornier Do 17M, P and Z

Country of origin: Germany.
Type: Three-seat, land-based medium bomber, (P) reconnaissance aircraft, (Z) four-seat medium bomber.
Dimensions: Wing span 59ft 0½in *18.02m*; length 52ft 9¾in *16.10m*, (Z) 51ft 9½in *15.79m*; height 14ft 11½in *4.56m*; wing area 592.02 sq ft *55.0m²*.
Weights: Empty (Z) 11,488lb *5210kg*; loaded 17,640lb *8000kg*, (P) 16,890lb

7660kg, (Z) 18,930lb *8585kg*.
Powerplant: Two BMW-Bramo 323A-1 Fafnir nine-cylinder radial engines each rated at 1000hp, (P) BMW 132N rated at 865hp, (Z) BMW-Bramo 323P Fafnir rated at 1000hp.
Performance: Maximum speed 255mph *410kph* at 13,120ft *4000m*, (P) 246mph *396kph* at 13,120ft; service ceiling 22,950ft *7000m*, (P) 20,340ft *6200m*; range

about 800 miles *1290km*.
Armament: Up to 2205lb *1000kg* of bombs in fuselage bay, plus three or (Z) six flexibly mounted 7.9mm MG 15 machine guns.
Service: First flight (Do 17 V1) late 1934, (V8) summer 1937, (Z-0) late 1938; service entry (M, P) early 1938, (Z) early 1939.

Plan view, Do 17M and P

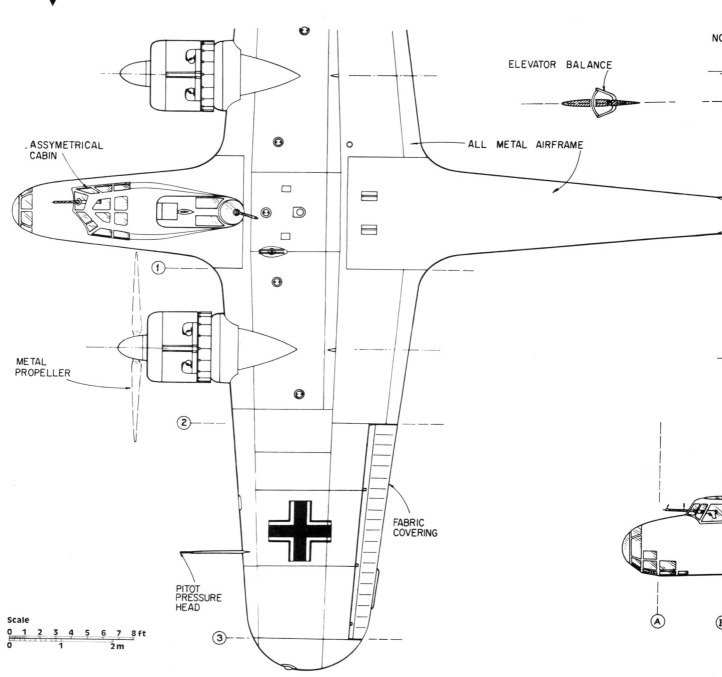

▲ A Do 17P shows its slim fuselage, which gave rise to the aircraft's nickname of 'The Flying Pencil'. Do 17s, mainly Zs, were active during the Battle of Britain.

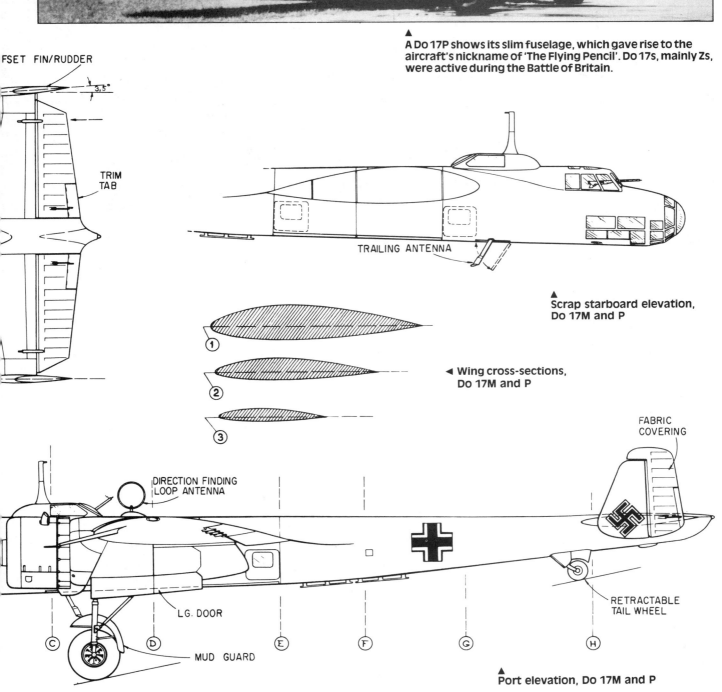

FSET FIN/RUDDER

3.5°

TRIM TAB

TRAILING ANTENNA

▲ Scrap starboard elevation, Do 17M and P

1

2

3

◀ Wing cross-sections, Do 17M and P

FABRIC COVERING

DIRECTION FINDING LOOP ANTENNA

LG. DOOR

MUD GUARD

RETRACTABLE TAIL WHEEL

C D E F G H

▲ Port elevation, Do 17M and P

  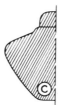

▲
Fuselage cross-sections, Do 17M and P

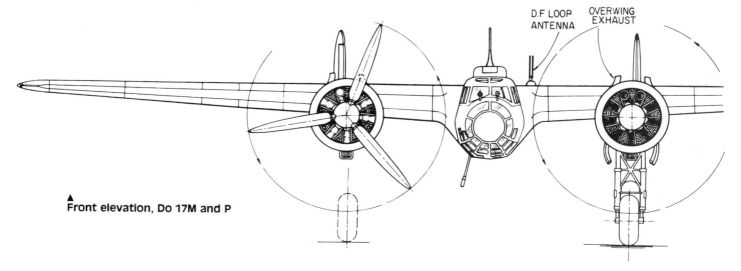

D.F LOOP ANTENNA

OVERWING EXHAUST

▲
Front elevation, Do 17M and P

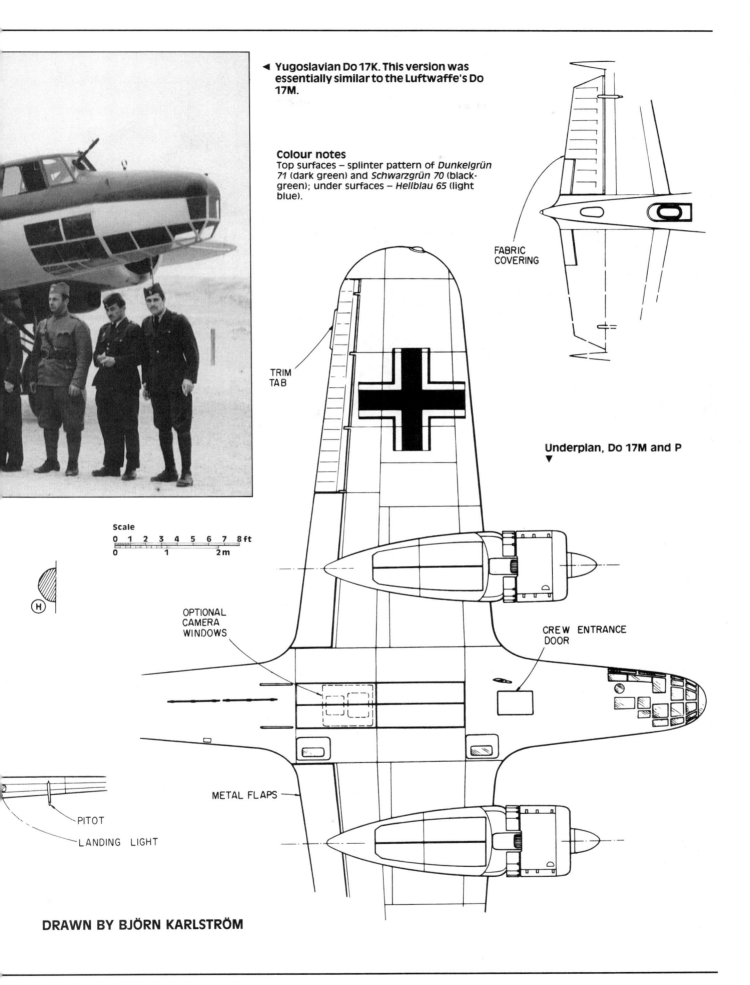

◄ **Yugoslavian Do 17K. This version was essentially similar to the Luftwaffe's Do 17M.**

Colour notes
Top surfaces – splinter pattern of *Dunkelgrün 71* (dark green) and *Schwarzgrün 70* (black-green); under surfaces – *Hellblau 65* (light blue).

FABRIC COVERING

TRIM TAB

Underplan, Do 17M and P
▼

OPTIONAL CAMERA WINDOWS

CREW ENTRANCE DOOR

METAL FLAPS

Scale
0 1 2 3 4 5 6 7 8 ft
0 1 2 m

PITOT

LANDING LIGHT

DRAWN BY BJÖRN KARLSTRÖM

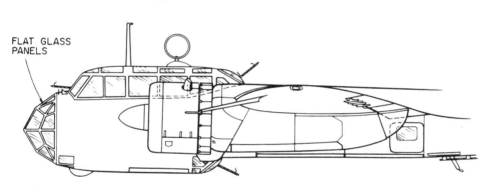

FLAT GLASS PANELS

▲ Scrap port elevation, Do 17Z

Scale

0 1 2 3 4 5 6 7 8 ft

0 1 2 m

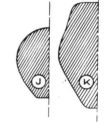

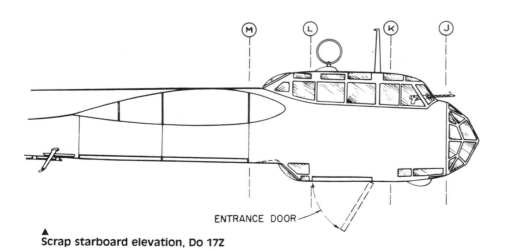

ENTRANCE DOOR

▲ Scrap starboard elevation, Do 17Z

▲ Fuselage cross-sections, Do 17Z

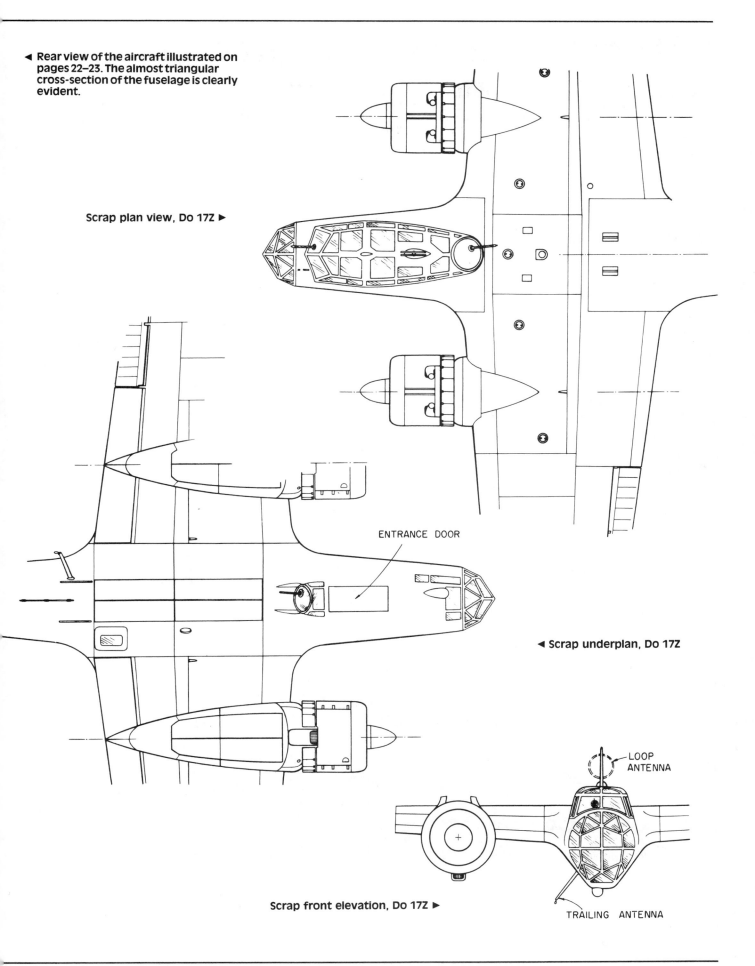

◄ Rear view of the aircraft illustrated on pages 22–23. The almost triangular cross-section of the fuselage is clearly evident.

Scrap plan view, Do 17Z ►

ENTRANCE DOOR

◄ Scrap underplan, Do 17Z

LOOP ANTENNA

TRAILING ANTENNA

Scrap front elevation, Do 17Z ►

Vickers-Armstrong Wellington B Mk I

Country of origin: Great Britain.
Type: Land-based medium bomber.
Dimensions: Wing span 86ft 2in *26.26m*;
length 64ft 7in *19.69m*; height 17ft 5in
5.31m; wing area 840 sq ft *78.04m²*.
Weights: Empty 18,556lb *8415kg*; loaded
25,800lb *11,701kg*.

Powerplant: Two Bristol Pegasus XVIII
radial engines each rated at 1050hp.
Performance: Maximum speed 235mph
378mph: service ceiling 19,000ft *5485m*;
range (normal) 1805 miles *2905km*.
Armament: Up to 4500lb *2040kg* of
bombs in fuselage bay, plus (later Mk Is)

six turret-mounted 0.303in machine
guns.
Service: First flight (prototype) 15 June
1936, (Mk I) 23 December 1937; service
entry February 1939.

DRAWN BY PETER G COOKSLEY

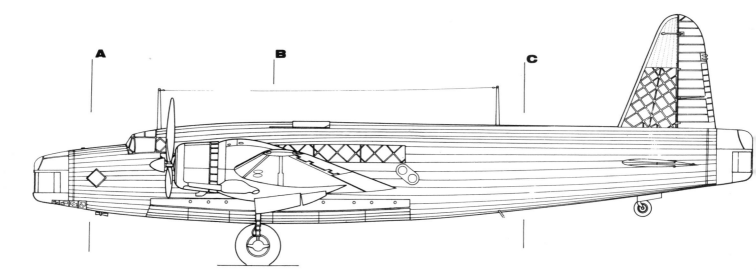

▲
Port elevation, B Mk I

Wellington Is of No 9 Squadron RAF. Later variants would be
equipped with nose and tail turrets and beam guns. Like its
stablemate the Wellesley, the 'Wimpey' utilised the geodetic
system of construction.
▼

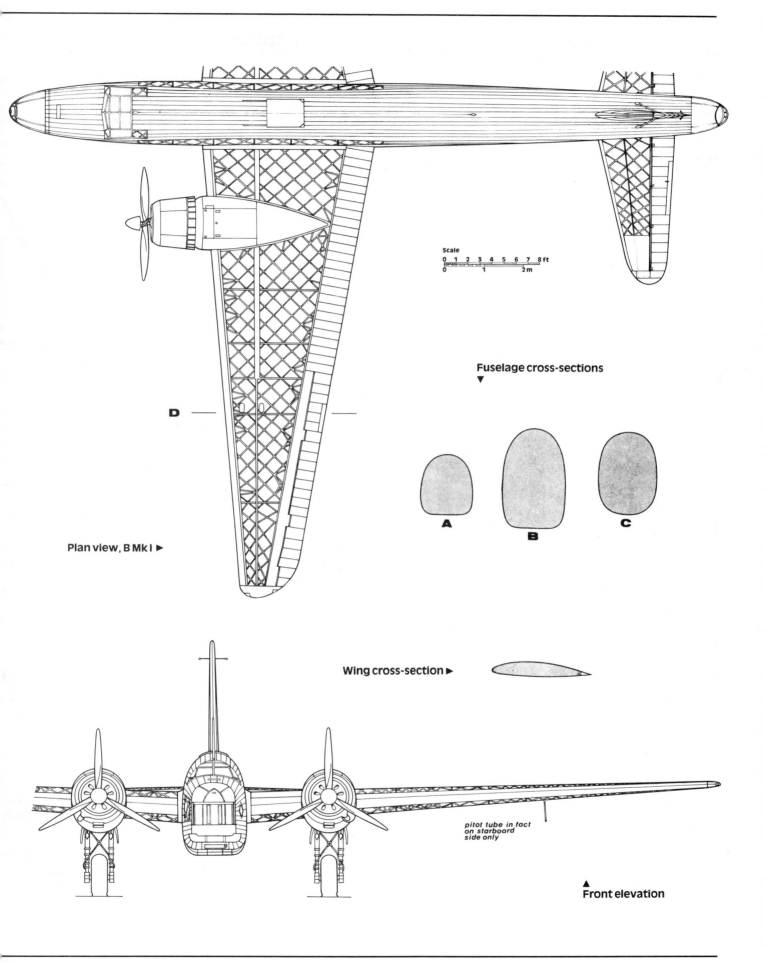

Plan view, B Mk I ►

Scale
0 1 2 3 4 5 6 7 8 ft
0 1 2 m

D

Fuselage cross-sections
▼

A   B   C

Wing cross-section ►

pitot tube in fact
on starboard
side only

▲
Front elevation

Boeing B-17E, F and G Fortress

Country of origin: USA.
Type: Land-based, high-altitude bomber.
Dimensions: Wing span 103ft 9in *31.62m*; length 73ft 10in *22.50m*, (G) 74ft 9in *22.78m*; height 19ft 1in *5.82m*; wing area 1420 sq ft *131.92m²*.
Weights: Empty 32,720lb *14,839kg*; normal loaded 49,500lb *22,449kg*; maximum 53,000lb *24,036kg*, (G) 60,000lb *27,211kg*.

Powerplant: Four Wright R-1820-65 Cyclone nine-cylinder radial engines each rated at 1200hp, (later F, G) R-1820-97 each rated at 1200hp.
Performance: Maximum speed 317mph *510kph* at 25,000ft *7620m*, (G) 295mph *475kph* at 25,000ft; time to 25,000ft, 41min; service ceiling 35,000ft *10,670m*; range (normal) 1100 miles *1770km*.

Armament: Normal bomb load 6000lb *2721kg*, maximum load 12,800lb *5805kg*; up to thirteen 0.5in Browning machine guns.
Service: First flight (Model 299) 28 July 1935, (Y1B-17) January 1937, (E) September 1941, (G) late 1942; service entry (B) June 1939.

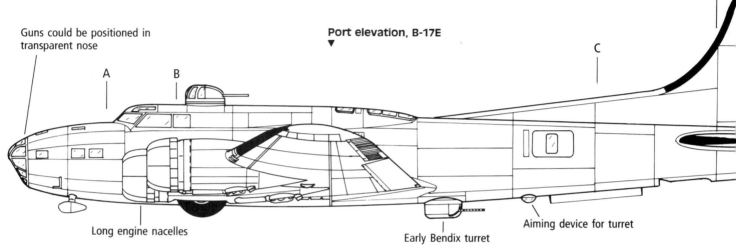

Guns could be positioned in transparent nose

A B

Port elevation, B-17E

C

D

Long engine nacelles

Early Bendix turret

Aiming device for turret

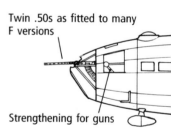

Twin .50s as fitted to many F versions

Strengthening for guns

▲ Early B-17 with inline engines. The Fortress took the major responsibility for the Allies' daylight bombing offensive against Germany during World War II.

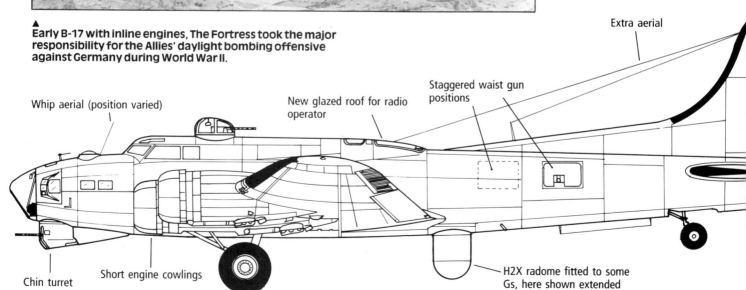

Whip aerial (position varied)

New glazed roof for radio operator

Staggered waist gun positions

Extra aerial

Chin turret

Short engine cowlings

H2X radome fitted to some Gs, here shown extended

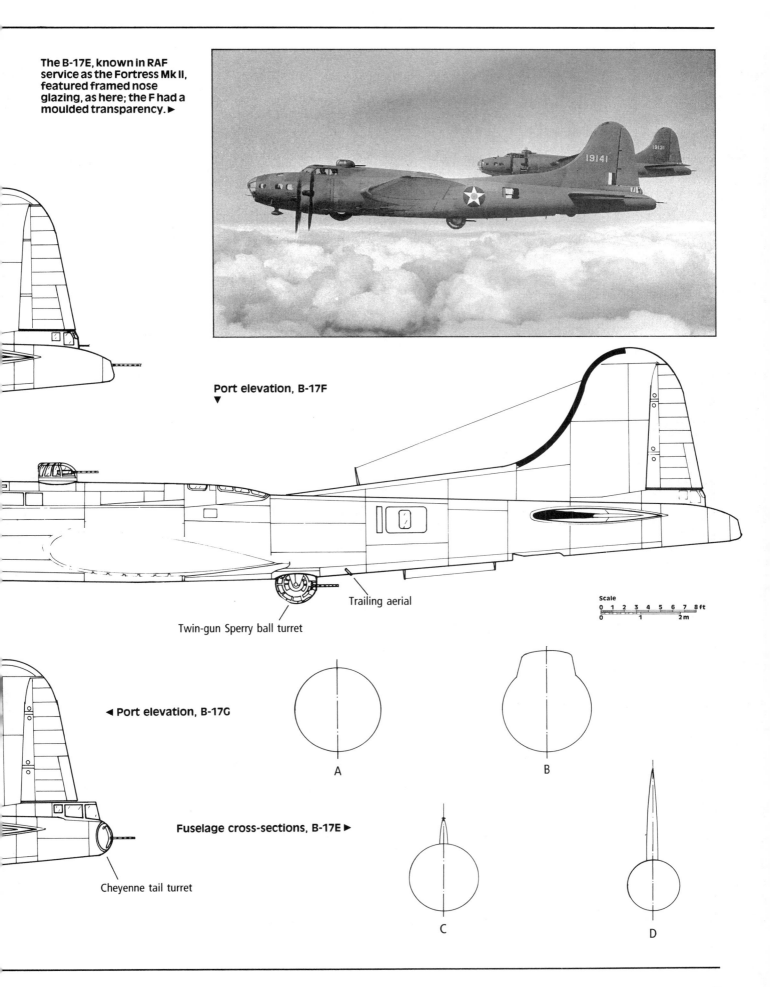

The B-17E, known in RAF service as the Fortress Mk II, featured framed nose glazing, as here; the F had a moulded transparency. ▶

Port elevation, B-17F
▼

Trailing aerial

Twin-gun Sperry ball turret

Scale
0 1 2 3 4 5 6 7 8 ft
0 1 2 m

◀ Port elevation, B-17G

A

B

Fuselage cross-sections, B-17E ▶

Cheyenne tail turret

C

D

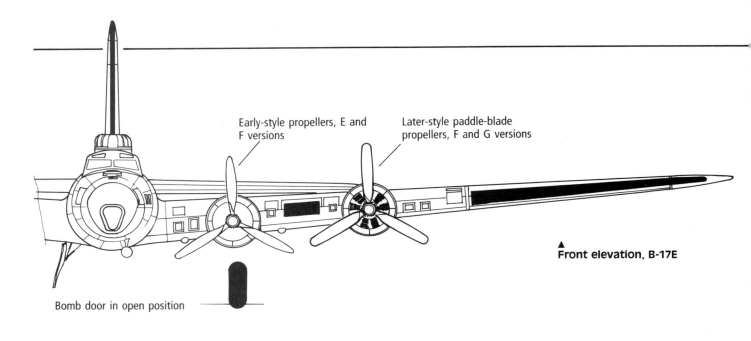

Early-style propellers, E and F versions

Later-style paddle-blade propellers, F and G versions

▲ **Front elevation, B-17E**

Bomb door in open position

◄ **Cockpit layout, B-17G.**

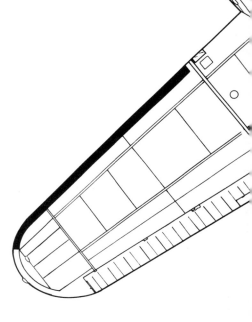

The B-17G's waist compartment, looking forward. Note the belly turret recess.

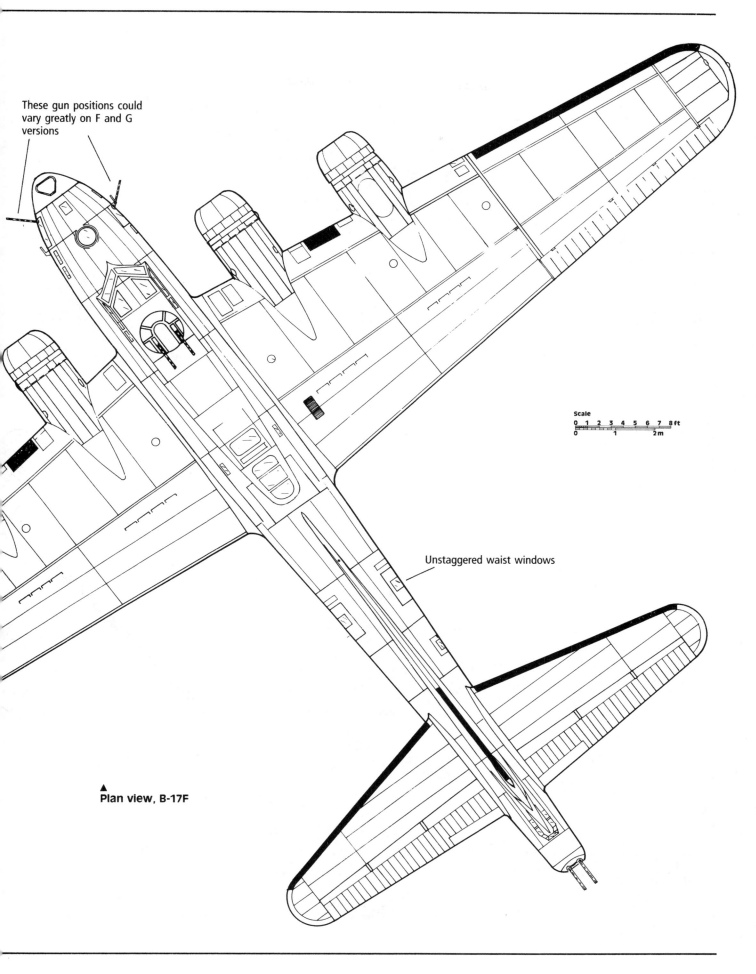

These gun positions could vary greatly on F and G versions

Scale

0 1 2 3 4 5 6 7 8 ft

0 1 2m

Unstaggered waist windows

▲
Plan view, B-17F

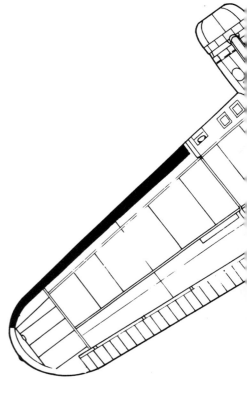

◄ The flight crew of 'Sweeney's Brats' pose beside their 8th Air Force B-17G. Note the cheek gun aft of the nose blister.

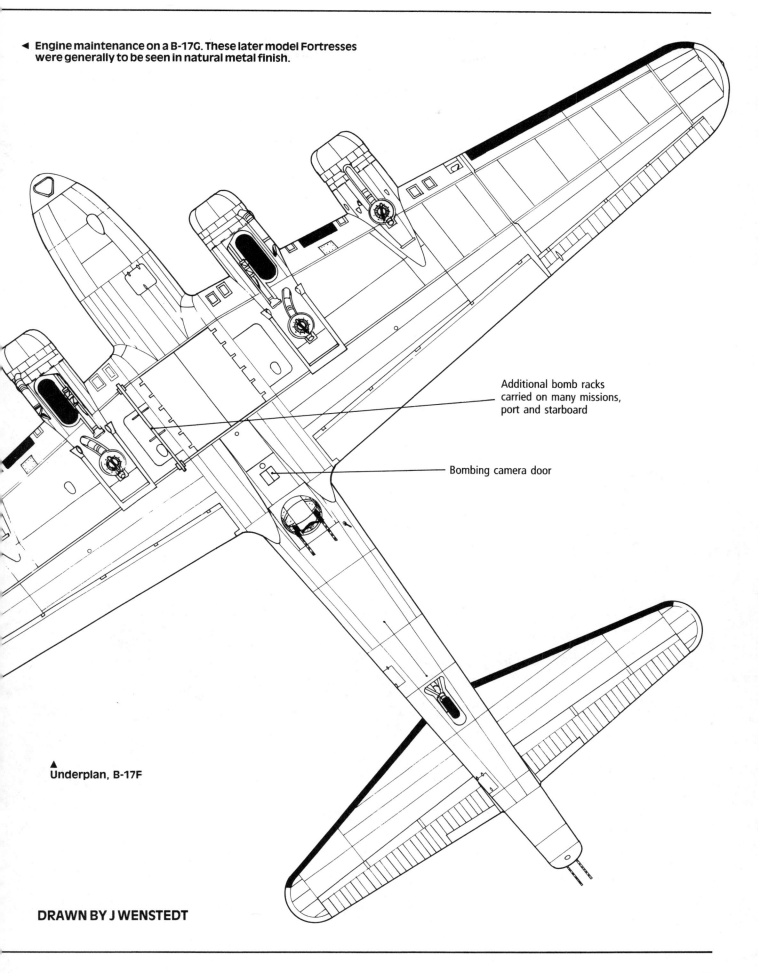

◄ Engine maintenance on a B-17G. These later model Fortresses were generally to be seen in natural metal finish.

Additional bomb racks carried on many missions, port and starboard

Bombing camera door

▲
Underplan, B-17F

DRAWN BY J WENSTEDT

Heinkel He 111H-2

Country of origin: Germany.
Type: Five-seat, land-based medium bomber.
Dimensions: Wing span 74ft 1¾in *22.60m*; length 53ft 9½in *16.40m*; height 13ft 1½in *4.00m*; wing area 931.1 sq ft *86.5m²*.
Weights: Empty equipped 19,139lb 8680kg; maximum 30,870lb *14,000kg*.
Powerplant: Two Junkers Jumo 211A-3 twelve-cylinder, liquid-cooled piston engines each rated at 1100hp.
Performance: Maximum speed 270mph *435kph* at 19,700ft *6000m*; time to 13,120ft *4000m*, 23.5min; service ceiling 27,890ft *8500m*; range about 1250 miles *2000km*.
Armament: Up to 4400lb *2000kg* of bombs in internal bay or 5510lb *2500kg* externally, plus (typically) six 7.9mm MG 15 machine guns.
Service: First flight (He 111a) 24 February 1935, (V19) January 1939; service entry (H-1) May 1939, (H-2) autumn 1939.

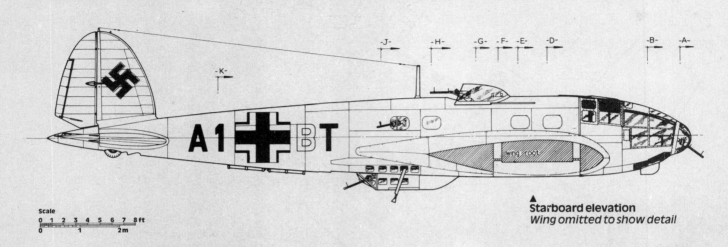

▲ **Starboard elevation**
Wing omitted to show detail

Scale
0 1 2 3 4 5 6 7 8 ft
0 1 2m

Not exactly an He 111, but a CASA 2111, a Spanish-built, Merlin-engined version of the famous German bomber, here seen painted up to represent the real thing for the film *Battle of Britain*.
▼

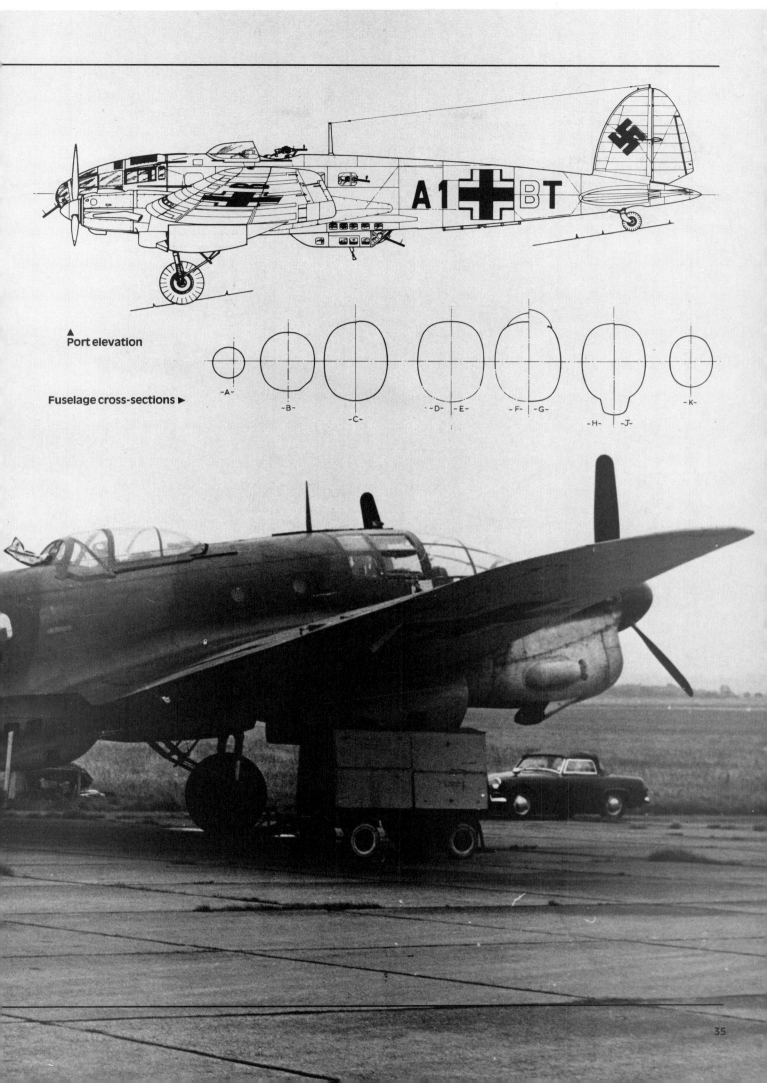

▲ Port elevation

Fuselage cross-sections ▶

~A~ ~B~ ~C~ ~D~ ~E~ ~F~ ~G~ ~H~ ~J~ ~K~

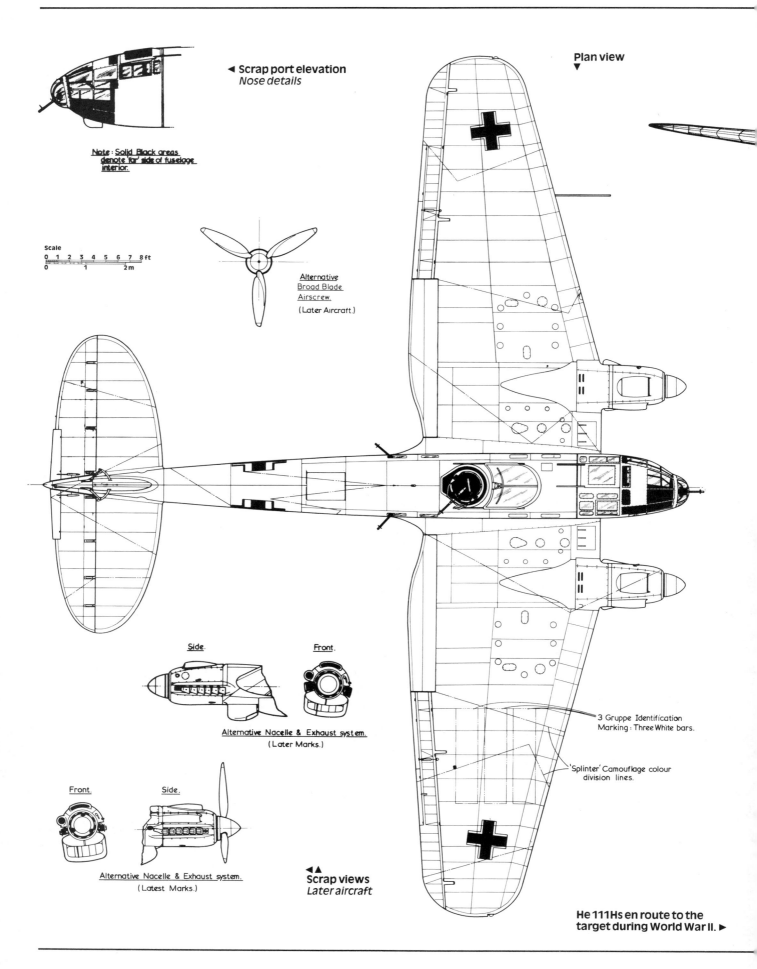

◀ **Scrap port elevation**
Nose details

Note: Solid Black areas denote 'far' side of fuselage interior.

Scale

Alternative
Broad Blade
Airscrew.
(Later Aircraft.)

Plan view
▼

Side.   Front.

Alternative Nacelle & Exhaust system.
(Later Marks.)

Front.   Side.

Alternative Nacelle & Exhaust system.
(Latest Marks.)

◀▲
Scrap views
Later aircraft

3 Gruppe Identification
Marking : Three White bars.

'Splinter' Camouflage colour
division lines.

**He 111Hs en route to the
target during World War II.** ▶

Front elevation
▼

**DRAWN BY J D CARRICK
TRACED BY C J NICHOLS**

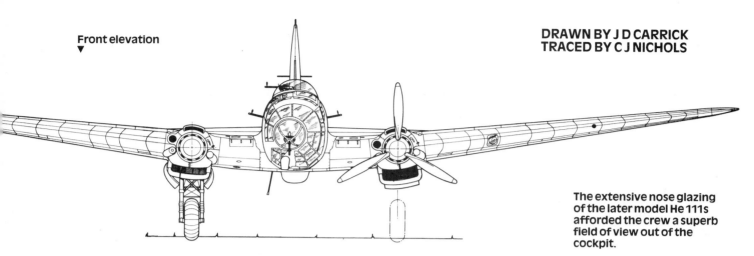

The extensive nose glazing of the later model He 111s afforded the crew a superb field of view out of the cockpit.

▲
The He 111P differed little from the early H versions but featured enlarged intakes on top of the engine cowlings.

Captured He 111 postwar with US and British insignia and a diminutive swastika on the tail.
▼

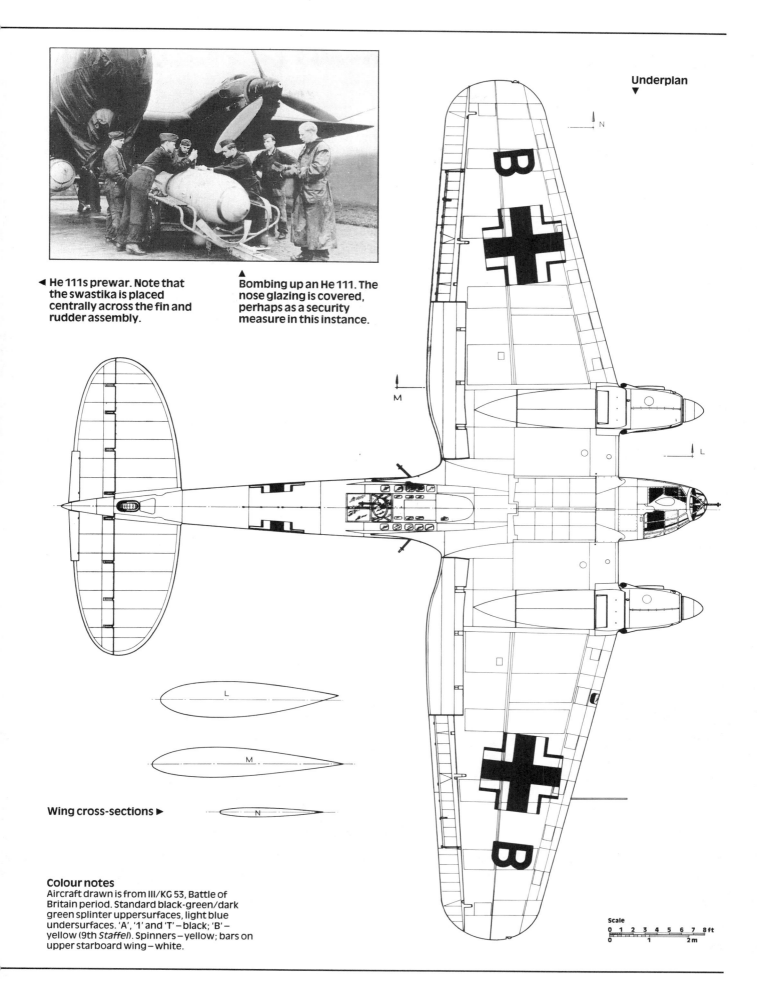

◄ He 111s prewar. Note that the swastika is placed centrally across the fin and rudder assembly.

▲
Bombing up an He 111. The nose glazing is covered, perhaps as a security measure in this instance.

Wing cross-sections ▶

Colour notes

Aircraft drawn is from III/KG 53, Battle of Britain period. Standard black-green/dark green splinter uppersurfaces, light blue undersurfaces. 'A', '1' and 'T' – black; 'B' – yellow (9th *Staffel*). Spinners – yellow; bars on upper starboard wing – white.

Scale
0 1 2 3 4 5 6 7 8 ft
0   1   2 m

Consolidated-Vultee B-24J Liberator, PB4Y-2 Privateer

Country of origin: USA.
Type: Long-range, land-based bomber or (PB4Y-2) patrol bomber.
Dimensions: Wing span 110ft *33.53m*; length 67ft 2in *20.47m*, (PB4Y-2) 74ft 0in *22.56m*; height 17ft 7½in *5.37m*, (PB4Y-2) 26ft 1in *7.95m*; wing area 1048 sq ft *97.36m².*
Weights: Empty 37,000lb *16,780kg*, (PB4Y-2) 41,000lb *18,594kg*; loaded

65,000lb *29,478kg.*
Powerplant: Four Pratt & Whitney R-1830-65 Twin Wasp fourteen-cylinder radial engines each rated at 1200hp, (PB4Y-2) R-1830-94 rated at 1200hp.
Performance: Maximum speed 297mph *478kph* at 25,000ft *7620m*, (PB4Y-2) 247mph *398kph*; initial climb rate (PB4Y-2) 800ft/min *244m/min*; service ceiling 28,000ft *8535m*, (PB4Y-2) 19,500ft

5945m; range (normal) 1540 miles *2480km*, (PB4Y-2) 2630 miles *4235km*.
Armament: Up to 8000lb *3628kg* of bombs in fuselage bays or up to 4000lb *1814kg* on wing racks, (PB4Y-2) up to 6000lb *2721kg* of ordnance in fuselage bays; ten or (PB4Y-2) twelve 0.5in Browning machine guns.
Service: First flight (XB-24) 29 December 1939, (XPB4Y-2) 20 September 1943.

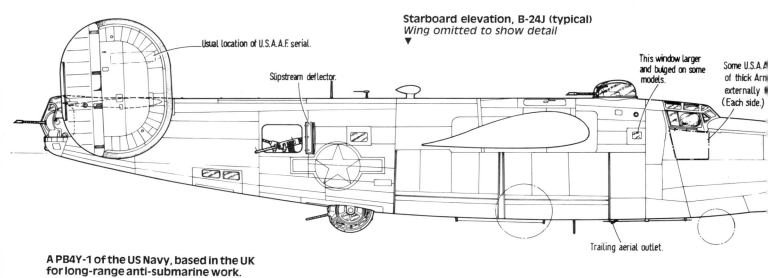

Starboard elevation, B-24J (typical)
Wing omitted to show detail
▼

Usual location of U.S.A.A.F. serial.

Slipstream deflector.

This window larger and bulged on some models.

Some U.S.A.A of thick Arm externally (Each side.)

Trailing aerial outlet.

A PB4Y-1 of the US Navy, based in the UK for long-range anti-submarine work.
▼

Preserved B-24D 'Strawberry Bitch'. Nose turrets were introduced with the G model.►

STRAWBERRY
BITCH

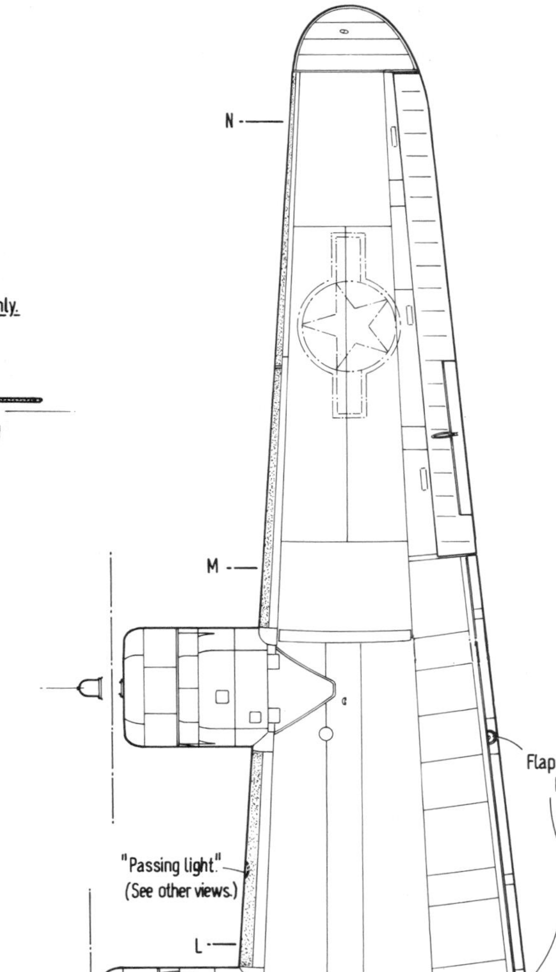

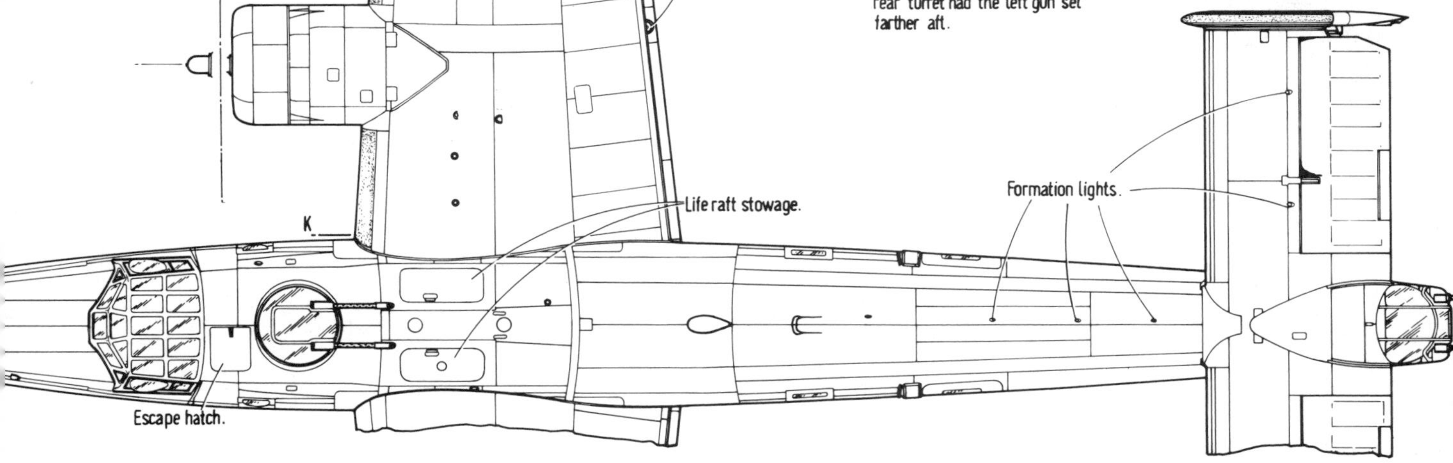

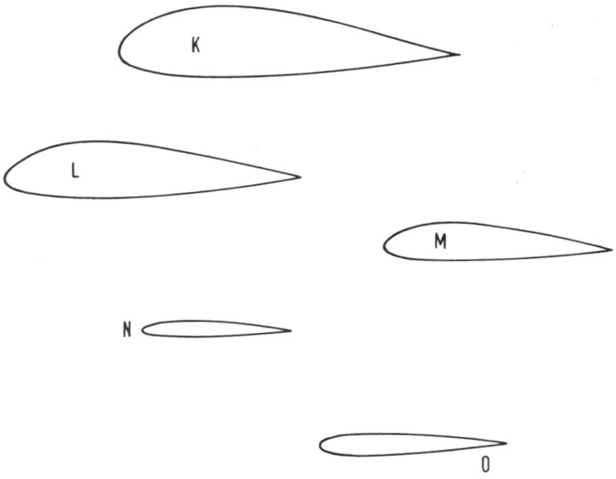

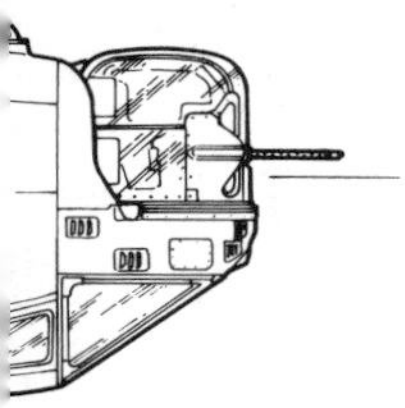

's had a 'slab'
te attached
ct the flight deck.
Eighth Air Force only.

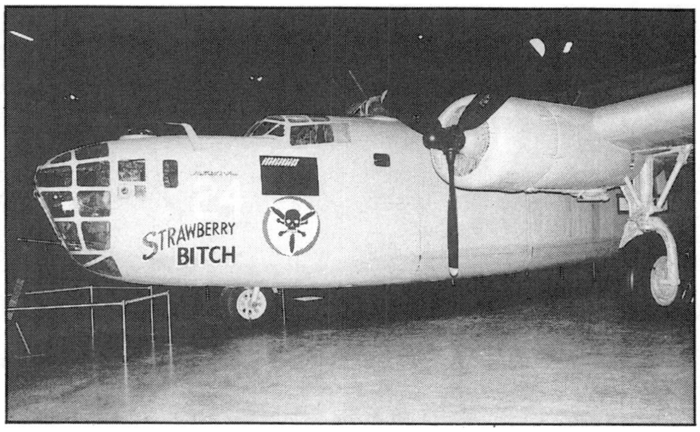

Scale
0 1 2 3 4 5 6 7 8 ft
0 1 2m

Plan view, B-24J ▼

N
M
L
K
Flap extension pulleys.
"Passing light." (See other views.)
Life raft stowage.
Escape hatch.
Formation lights.
* A number of batches of early aircraft fitted with a 'Consolidated' rear turret had the left gun set farther aft.

DRAWN BY K A MERRICK
TRACED BY A A P LLOYD

Wing and tailplane sections, B-24J ▼

K
L
M
N
O

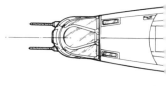

◄ One of the first RAF Liberators, originally produced to fulfil a French order.

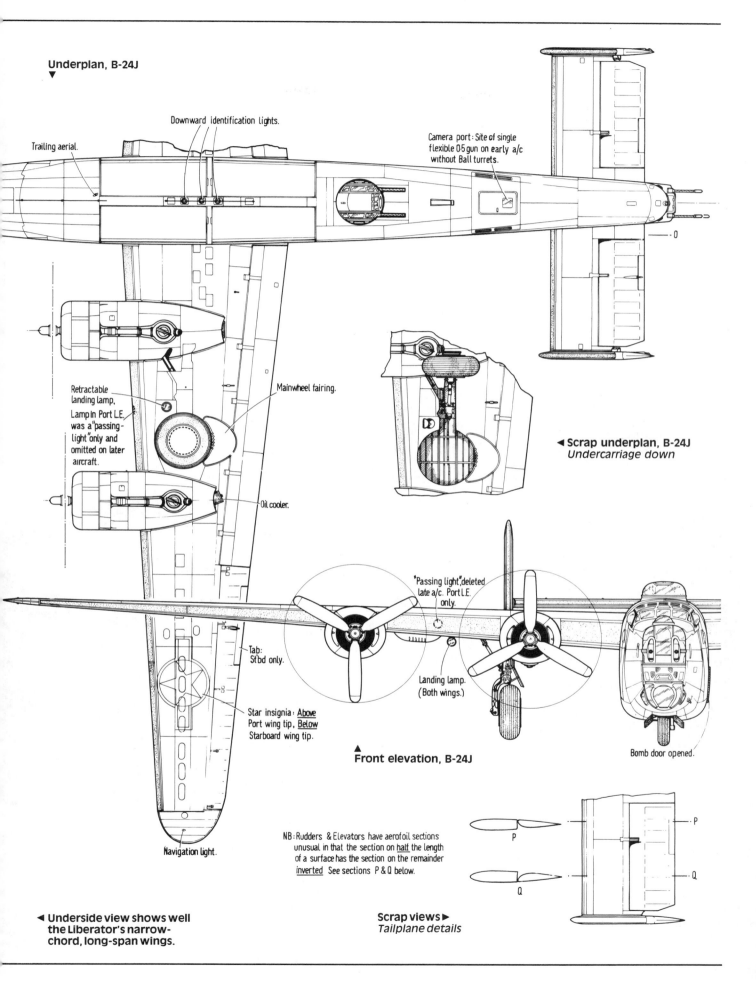

Underplan, B-24J

Trailing aerial.

Downward identification lights.

Camera port: Site of single flexible 0.5 gun on early a/c without Ball turrets.

Retractable landing lamp. Lamp in Port L.E. was a "passing-light" only and omitted on later aircraft.

Mainwheel fairing.

Oil cooler.

◄ Scrap underplan, B-24J
Undercarriage down

Tab: St'bd only.

Star insignia: <u>Above</u> Port wing tip, <u>Below</u> Starboard wing tip.

"Passing light" deleted late a/c. Port L.E. only.

Landing lamp. (Both wings.)

Bomb door opened.

Navigation light.

Front elevation, B-24J

NB: Rudders & Elevators have aerofoil sections unusual in that the section on <u>half</u> the length of a surface has the section on the remainder <u>inverted</u> See sections P & Q below.

P

Q

P

Q

◄ **Underside view shows well the Liberator's narrow-chord, long-span wings.**

Scrap views ►
Tailplane details

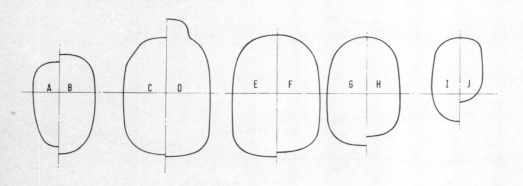

▲ Fuselage cross-sections, B-24J

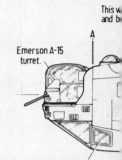

This w...
and b...

Emerson A-15 turret.

A

Not all B-24Js had these glazed panels.

An RAF Liberator Mk II, which had no US equivalent. Many of these aircraft were converted for use as long-range transports.
▼

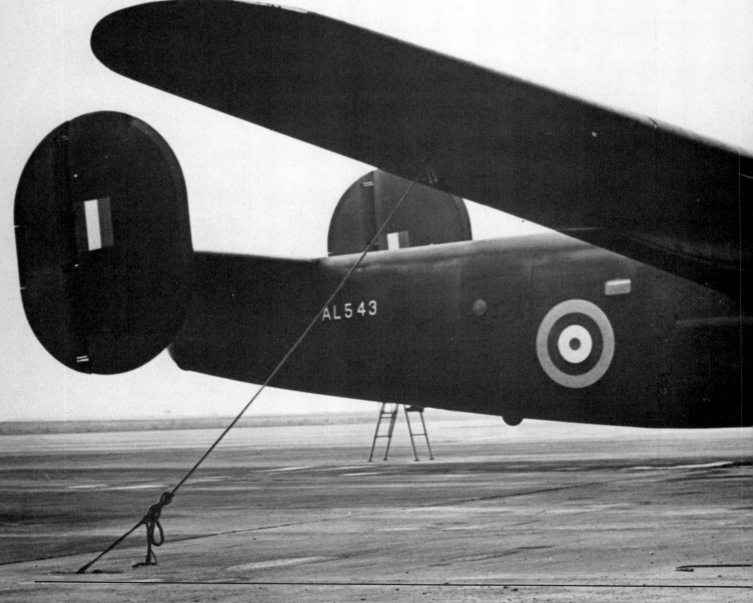

AL543

Port elevation, B-24J
▼

Aircraft in 'parked' configuration, Ball turret retracted, Tail skid extended, waist panels in place.

Navigation light.

Martin 250 CE-15 turret.

Escape hatch on Duxford a/c.

Motor Products MPC 5800-5 turret.

Window: Port only.

Bomb release light.

Not all aircraft had this type of Nosewheel doors, some retracted inwardly and did not show, but revealed a mudguard on the upper half of the nosewheel.

Briggs A-13 Retractable turret.

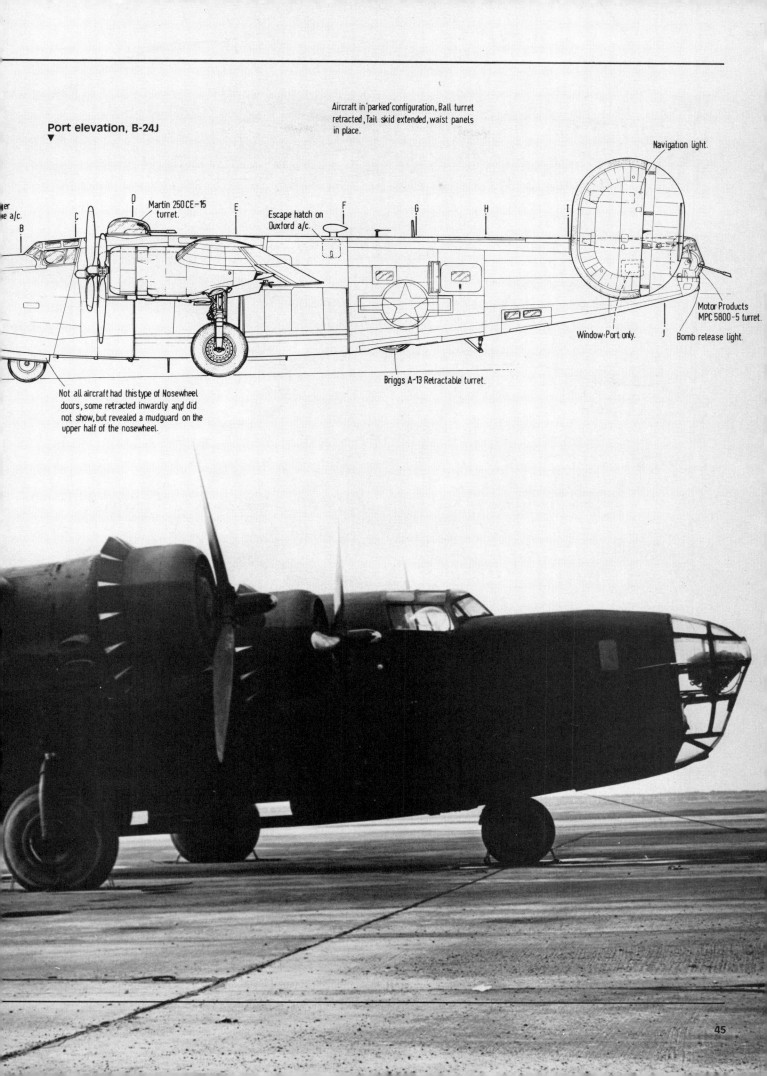

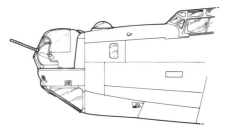

MPC 5800-5 Nose & Tail turrets, Martin 250 CE-5 Top turret.
(Lower profile.) & Briggs A-13 Ball turret.

▲
Scrap port elevation
B-24J-30 and Liberator Mk IV

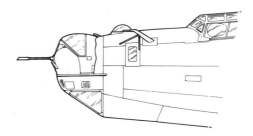

▲
Scrap port elevation
B-24J-5 and Liberator Mk VI

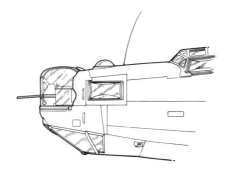

▲
Scrap port elevation
B-24L-20 and Liberator Mk VIII

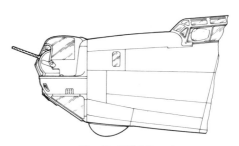

Alternative PB4Y-2 Nose using
MPC 5800-5 Turret. (As B-24J).

▲
Scrap port elevation, PB4Y-2
Alternative nose configuration

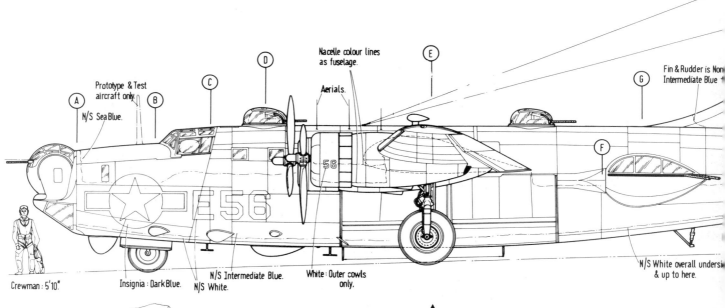

Nacelle colour lines
as fuselage.

Aerials.

Prototype & Test
aircraft only.

N/S Sea Blue.

Fin & Rudder is Non
Intermediate Blue

N/S Intermediate Blue.
N/S White.

Insignia : Dark Blue.

White: Outer cowls
only.

N/S White overall undersi
& up to here.

Crewman : 5'10."

▲
Port elevation, PB4Y-2

SCRAP ELEVATION : NOSEWHEEL.
Alternative inward folding wheel doors.

Fin cross-sections ▶

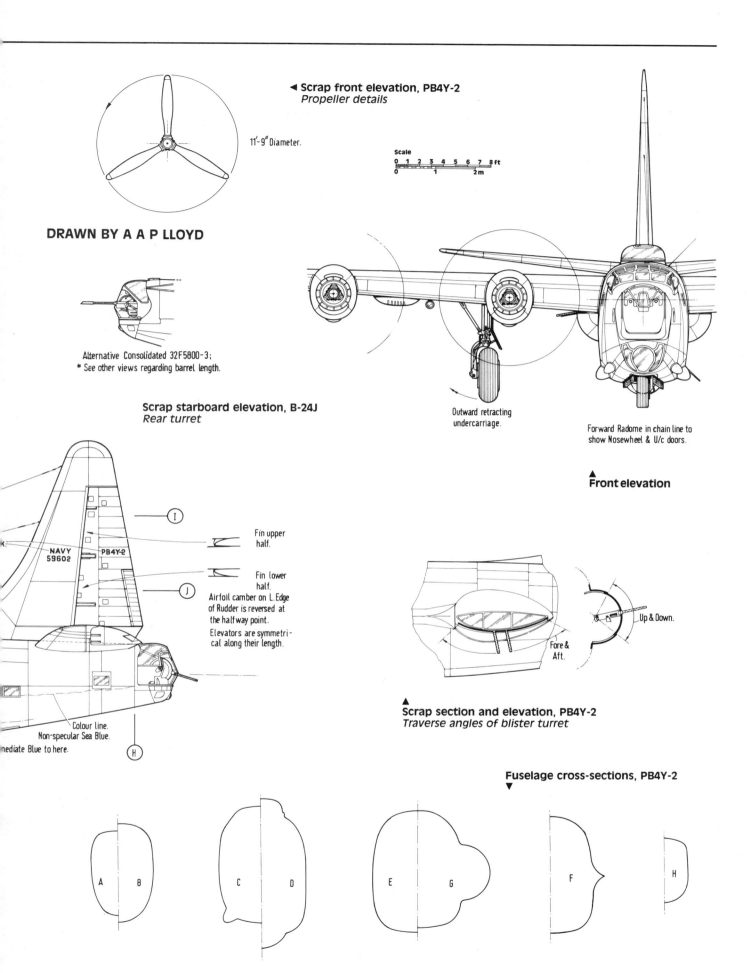

◄ **Scrap front elevation, PB4Y-2**
Propeller details

11'-9" Diameter.

Scale
0 1 2 3 4 5 6 7 8 ft
0   1   2m

DRAWN BY A A P LLOYD

Alternative Consolidated 32F5800-3;
* See other views regarding barrel length.

Scrap starboard elevation, B-24J
Rear turret

Outward retracting
undercarriage.

Forward Radome in chain line to
show Nosewheel & U/c doors.

▲
Front elevation

Fin upper
half.

Fin lower
half.
Airfoil camber on L.Edge
of Rudder is reversed at
the half way point.
Elevators are symmetri-
cal along their length.

NAVY
59602   PB4Y-2

Up & Down.

Fore &
Aft.

▲
Scrap section and elevation, PB4Y-2
Traverse angles of blister turret

Colour line.
Non-specular Sea Blue.
nediate Blue to here.

Fuselage cross-sections, PB4Y-2
▼

A B   C D   E G   F   H

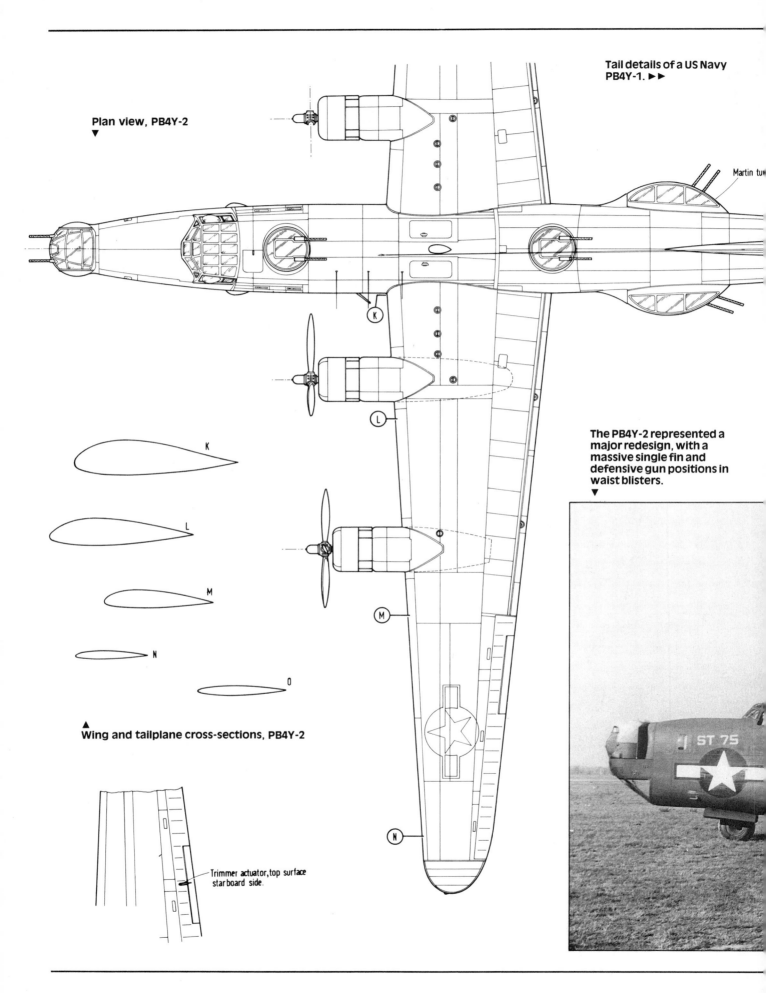

Tail details of a US Navy PB4Y-1. ►►

Plan view, PB4Y-2
▼

Martin tu

K

L

M

N

O

▲
Wing and tailplane cross-sections, PB4Y-2

Trimmer actuator, top surface
starboard side.

K

L

M

N

The PB4Y-2 represented a major redesign, with a massive single fin and defensive gun positions in waist blisters.
▼

ST 75

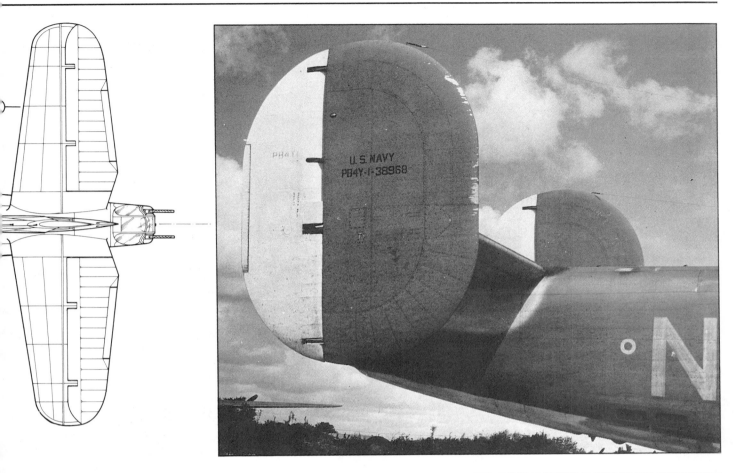

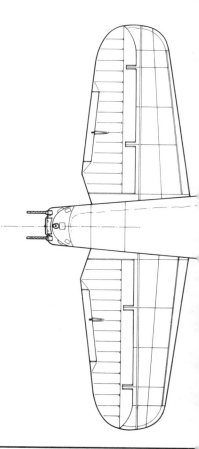

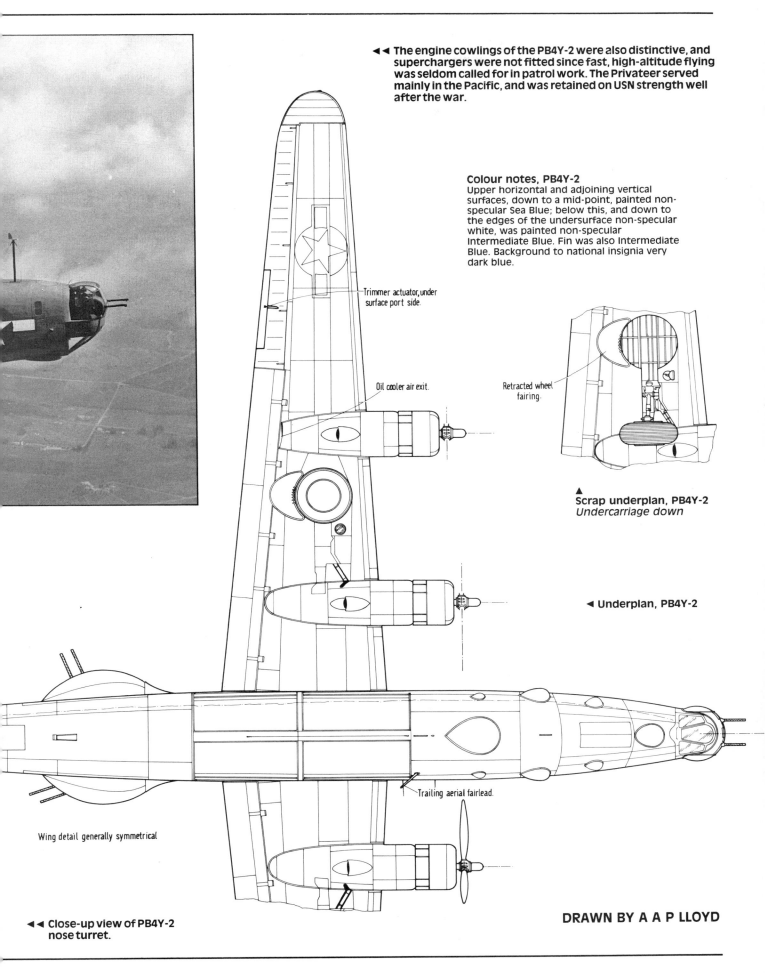

◄◄ The engine cowlings of the PB4Y-2 were also distinctive, and superchargers were not fitted since fast, high-altitude flying was seldom called for in patrol work. The Privateer served mainly in the Pacific, and was retained on USN strength well after the war.

Colour notes, PB4Y-2
Upper horizontal and adjoining vertical surfaces, down to a mid-point, painted non-specular Sea Blue; below this, and down to the edges of the undersurface non-specular white, was painted non-specular Intermediate Blue. Fin was also Intermediate Blue. Background to national insignia very dark blue.

Trimmer actuator, under surface port side.

Oil cooler air exit.

Retracted wheel fairing.

▲ **Scrap underplan, PB4Y-2**
Undercarriage down

◄ **Underplan, PB4Y-2**

Trailing aerial fairlead.

Wing detail generally symmetrical

◄◄ **Close-up view of PB4Y-2 nose turret.**

DRAWN BY A A P LLOYD

Handley Page Halifax B Mks I–IX

Country of origin: Great Britain.
Type: Land-based heavy bomber.
Dimensions: Wing span 98ft 8in *30.07m*, (late Mk III, Mks V–IX) 103ft 8in *31.60m*; length 70ft 1in *21.36m*, (late Mk III, Mks V–VII) 71ft 7in *21.82m*, (Mk VIII) 73ft 7in *22.43m*; height 21ft 7in *6.58m*; wing area (late Mk III, Mks V–IX) 1275 sq ft *118.45m²*.
Weights: Empty (Mk I Srs I) 33,860lb *15,356kg*, (Mk II Srs IA) 35,370lb *16,041kg*, (Mk III) 38,239lb *17,342kg*; loaded (Mk I Srs I) 55,000lb *24,943kg*, (Mk II Srs IA) 63,000lb

28,571kg, (Mk III) 65,000lb *29,478kg*.
Powerplant: (Mk I Srs I) Four Rolls-Royce Merlin X V12, liquid-cooled piston engines each rated at 1280hp, (Mk II Srs IA) Merlin 22 rated at 1390hp, (Mk III, Mk VII) Bristol Hercules XVI rated at 1615hp, (Mk VI) Bristol Hercules 100 rated at 1800hp.
Performance: Maximum speed (Mk I Srs I) 265mph *427kph*, (Mk II Srs IA) 272mph *438kph*, (Mk III) over 270mph *435kph*; range about 3000 miles *4830km*.

Armament: (Mks I–VII) Up to 14,500lb *6576kg* of bombs in fuselage and wing bays, plus (Mk I Srs I) six turret-mounted 0.303in and two flexibly mounted 0.303in machine guns or (Mk II Srs IA, Mks III–VII) eight turret-mounted and one flexibly mounted 0.303in machine guns; (Mk VIII) none.
Service: First flight (prototype) 25 October 1939, (Mk II) 19 March 1941, (Mk VI) 10 October 1944; service entry (Mk I) 23 November 1940.

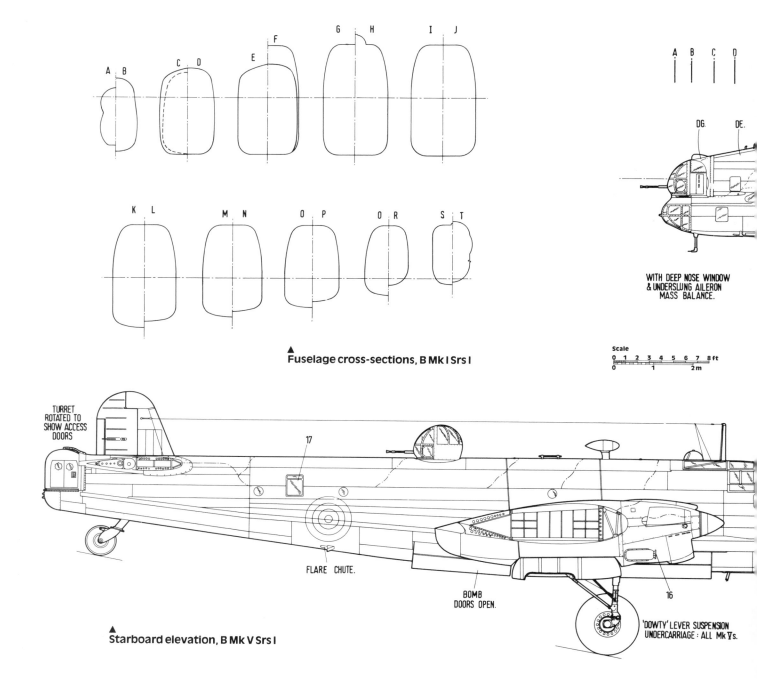

▲ Fuselage cross-sections, B Mk I Srs I

WITH DEEP NOSE WINDOW & UNDERSLUNG AILERON MASS BALANCE.

Scale

TURRET ROTATED TO SHOW ACCESS DOORS

17

FLARE CHUTE.

BOMB DOORS OPEN.

16

'DOWTY' LEVER SUSPENSION UNDERCARRIAGE : ALL Mk Vs.

▲ Starboard elevation, B Mk V Srs I

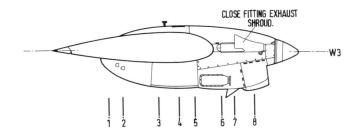

CLOSE FITTING EXHAUST SHROUD.

W3

1 2 3 4 5 6 7 8

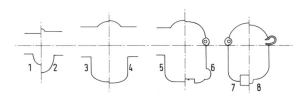

1 2 3 4 5 6 7 8

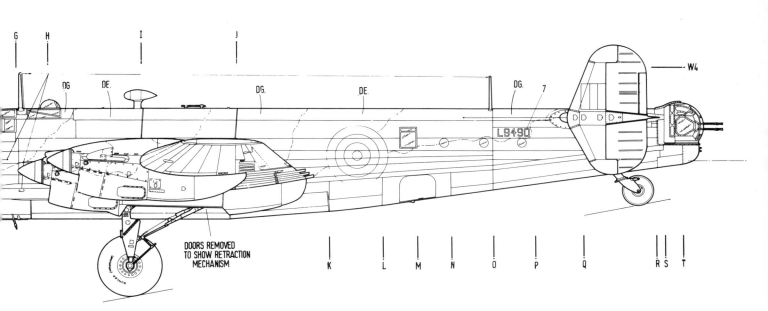

G H I J

DG. DE. DG. DE. DG. 7

W4

L9490

DOORS REMOVED TO SHOW RETRACTION MECHANISM

K L M N O P Q R S T

▲
Port elevation, B Mk I Srs I

Halifax Mk I of No 76 Squadron, showing early fin shape. Somewhat overshadowed by the Lancaster, the Halifax nevertheless made a major contribution to the RAF's bombing campaign against Germany.
▼

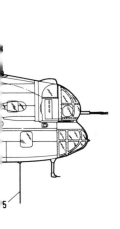

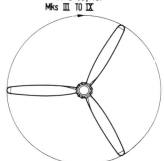

DE HAVILLAND HYDROMATIC: 13' 0" DIA.
TYPE 55/18.
Mks III TO IX

Numerical key

1. ½in wide frame, 4in × 5.4in with 2in letters – 'Trestle here'. 2. '24 volt' – 2in numerals, 1in letters, yellow. 3. 'Jack here' – 1in letters, yellow. 4. 'No step' – black. 5. ½in wide frame, 4in × 4in with 2in letters in yellow – 'Trestle here'. 6. 'Lift here' – 1in letters, yellow. 7. Figures 8in high × 5in wide × 1in stroke, 1½in spacing – Dull Red on later marks. 8. 'To open pull handle' – yellow. 9. '2¼ gals oil 6¼ gals air space' – black on yellow background. 10.

Turret balance flap. 11. Internal frame. 12. Dinghy stowage, port wing only (both wings C Mk VIII and A Mk IX); Dull Red sealing strip around edges. 13. Windscreen de-icing spray nozzles. 14. Lorenz B/A aerial. 15. Vertical camera aperture. 16. Ice guards. 17. Beam gun hatch. 18. Escape hatch. 19. Cable cutters – red. 20. Cable cutter ramp. 21. Fuel tank vent. 22. Bulbous nose modification. 23. Flap jack shroud. 24. Trailing aerial fairlead. 25. Whip aerial.

N.B. ALL PROPELLERS BLACK
WITH YELLOW TIPS.

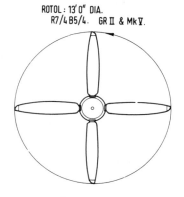

ROTOL : 13' 0" DIA.
R7/4 B5/4.   GR II & Mk V.

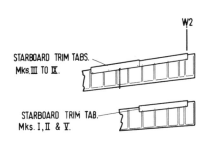

STARBOARD TRIM TABS.
Mks. III TO IX.

STARBOARD TRIM TAB.
Mks. I, II & V.

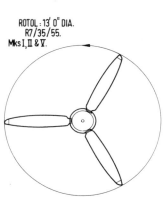

ROTOL : 13' 0" DIA.
R7/35/55.
Mks I, II & V.

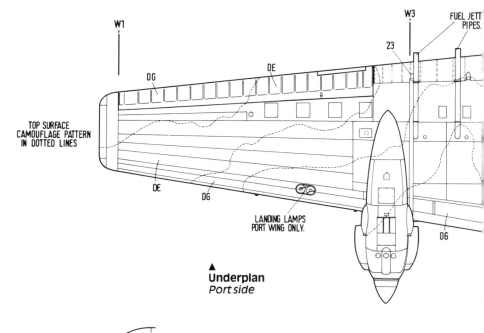

TOP SURFACE
CAMOUFLAGE PATTERN
IN DOTTED LINES

LANDING LAMPS
PORT WING ONLY.

▲ **Underplan**
Port side

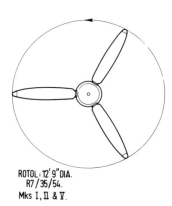

ROTOL : 12' 9" DIA.
R7/35/54.
Mks I, II & V.

UNDERSIDE.

EXTENDED
WING TIP.

TOPSIDE.

Scale

▲ **Scrap front elevations**
Propeller details

DRAWN BY K A MERRICK
TRACED BY A A P LLOYD

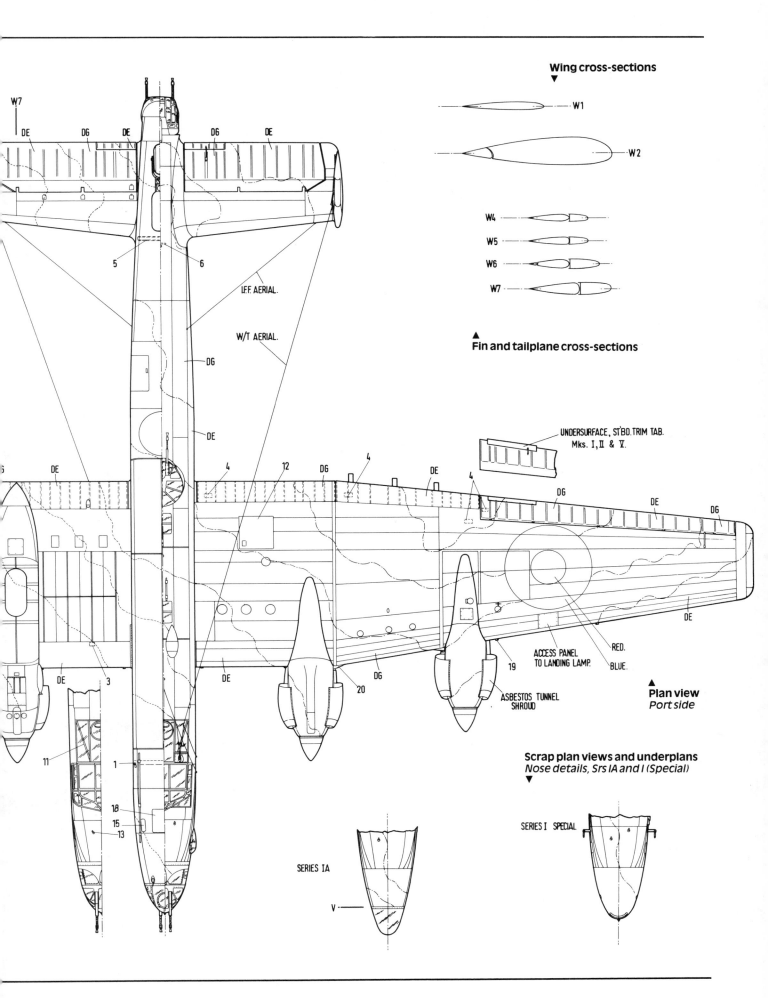

Wing cross-sections ▼

W1

W2

W4

W5

W6

W7

▲ **Fin and tailplane cross-sections**

W7

DE

DG   DE   DG   DE

5   6

I.F.F. AERIAL.

W/T AERIAL.

DG

DE

DE

DG

DE   4   12   DG   4   DE

4

UNDERSURFACE, ST'BD. TRIM TAB.
Mks. I, II & V.

DG

DE   DG

DE

RED.

ACCESS PANEL
TO LANDING LAMP.   BLUE.

19

DE   DE   DG

DE   3

DE   20

ASBESTOS TUNNEL
SHROUD

▲ **Plan view**
Port side

11   1

18

15

13

Scrap plan views and underplans
Nose details, Srs IA and I (Special)
▼

SERIES IA

V

SERIES I SPECIAL

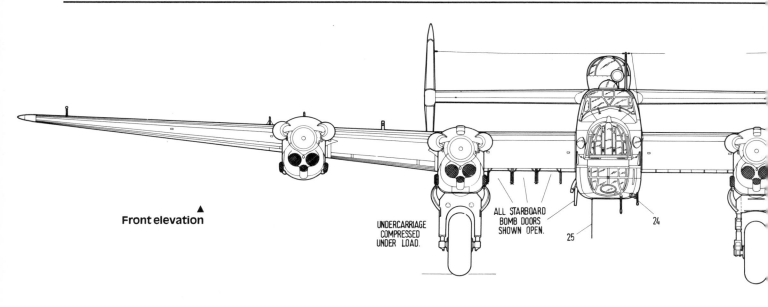

Front elevation ▲

UNDERCARRIAGE
COMPRESSED
UNDER LOAD.

ALL STARBOARD
BOMB DOORS
SHOWN OPEN.

24

25

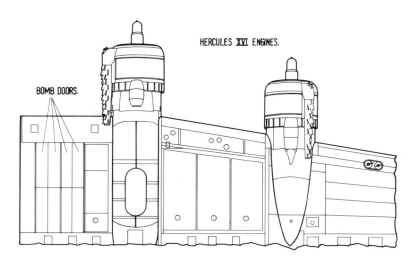

HERCULES XVI ENGINES.

BOMB DOORS.

Scrap front elevations
Engine details
▼

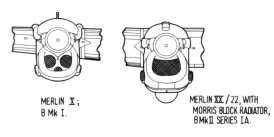

MERLIN X;
B Mk I.

MERLIN XX / 22, WITH
MORRIS BLOCK RADIATOR,
B Mk II SERIES IA.

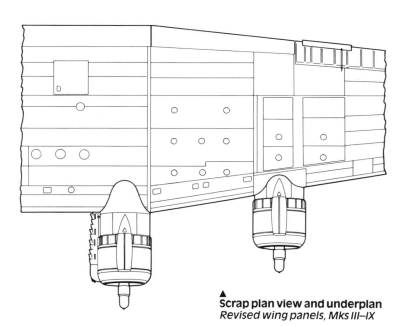

Scrap plan view and underplan ▲
Revised wing panels, Mks III–IX

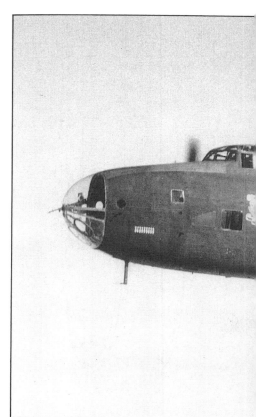

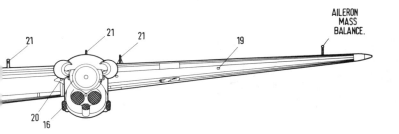

AILERON MASS BALANCE.

21   21   21   19

20   16

DOWTY UNDERCARRIAGE OF Mk.Ⅴ; UNLOADED.

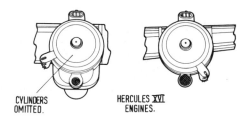

CYLINDERS OMITTED.

HERCULES ⅩⅥ ENGINES.

▲ **Scrap front elevations**
Engine details

Scrap port elevation and cross-sections
Hercules XVI engine nacelle
▼ ▶

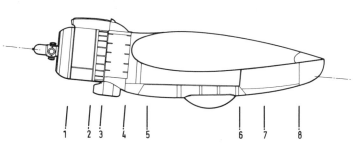

1   2   3   4   5   6   7   8

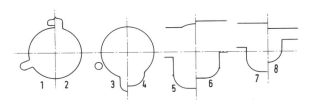

1   2   3   4   5   6   7   8

A No 35 Squadron Mk II, with H2S fairing well in evidence. Note mission symbols and pilot Alec Cranswick's crest on forward fuselage.
▼

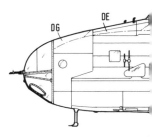

▲
Another No 76 Squadron B Mk I, showing camouflage boundary variations compared to L9530 depicted on page 53.

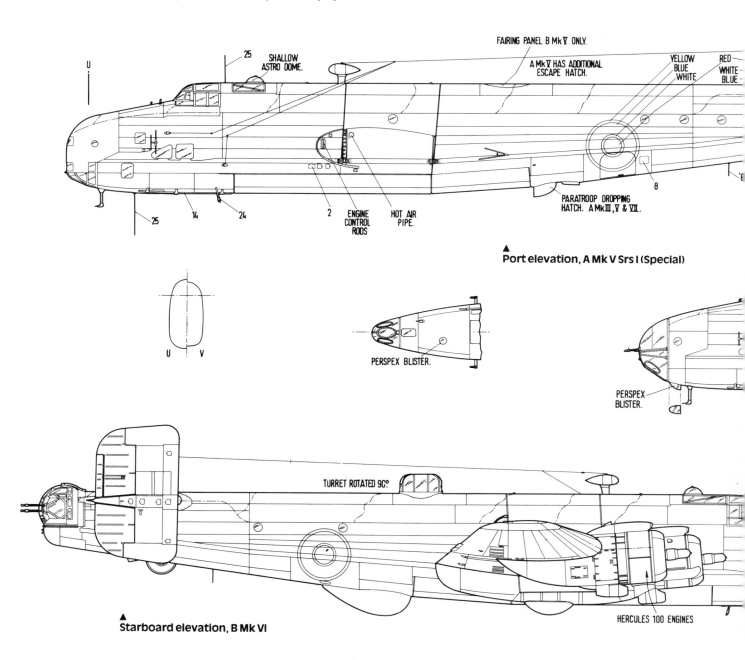

SHALLOW ASTRO DOME.

FAIRING PANEL B Mk V ONLY.

A Mk V HAS ADDITIONAL ESCAPE HATCH.

YELLOW
BLUE
WHITE

RED
WHITE
BLUE

25

U

14

24

2

ENGINE CONTROL RODS

HOT AIR PIPE.

25

8

PARATROOP DROPPING HATCH. A Mk III, V & VII.

▲
Port elevation, A Mk V Srs I (Special)

U   V

PERSPEX BLISTER.

PERSPEX BLISTER.

TURRET ROTATED 90°?

HERCULES 100 ENGINES

▲
Starboard elevation, B Mk VI

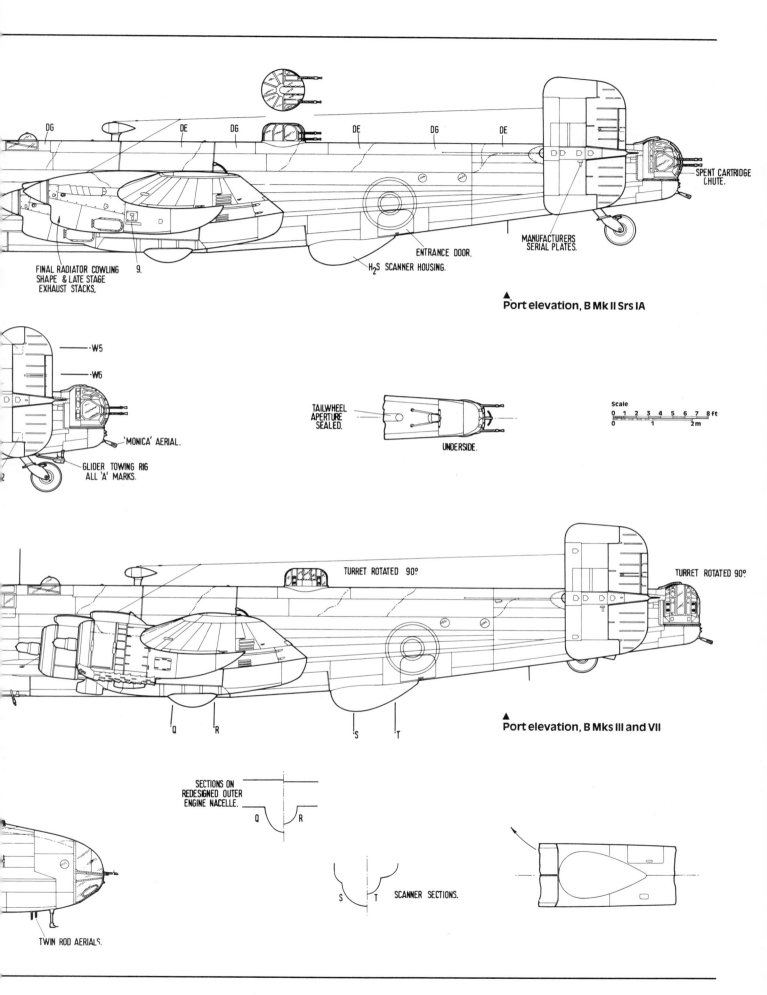

DG   DE   DG   DE   DG   DE

SPENT CARTRIDGE CHUTE.

FINAL RADIATOR COWLING SHAPE & LATE STAGE EXHAUST STACKS.

9.

ENTRANCE DOOR.

H₂S SCANNER HOUSING.

MANUFACTURERS SERIAL PLATES.

▲ Port elevation, B Mk II Srs IA

W5
W6

'MONICA' AERIAL.

GLIDER TOWING RIG ALL 'A' MARKS.

TAILWHEEL APERTURE SEALED.

UNDERSIDE.

Scale
0 1 2 3 4 5 6 7 8 ft
0   1   2m

TURRET ROTATED 90°

TURRET ROTATED 90°

▲ Port elevation, B Mks III and VII

Q   R   S   T

SECTIONS ON REDESIGNED OUTER ENGINE NACELLE.

Q   R

S   T   SCANNER SECTIONS.

TWIN ROD AERIALS.

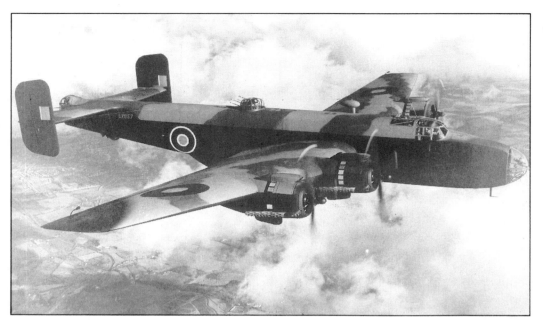

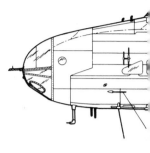

◄ One of the best-known photographs of a Halifax B.III, with Hercules radials.

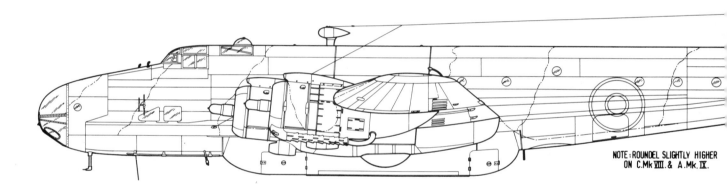

NOTE: ROUNDEL SLIGHTLY HIGHER ON C.Mk VIII. & A.Mk. IX.

▲ Port elevation, C Mk VIII

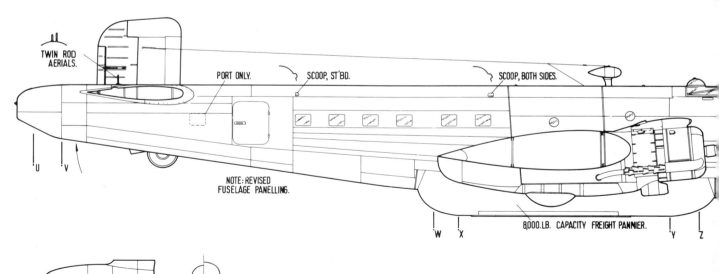

TWIN ROD AERIALS.

PORT ONLY.

SCOOP, ST'BD.

SCOOP, BOTH SIDES.

NOTE: REVISED FUSELAGE PANELLING.

8,000.LB. CAPACITY FREIGHT PANNIER.

▲ Starboard elevation, Halton

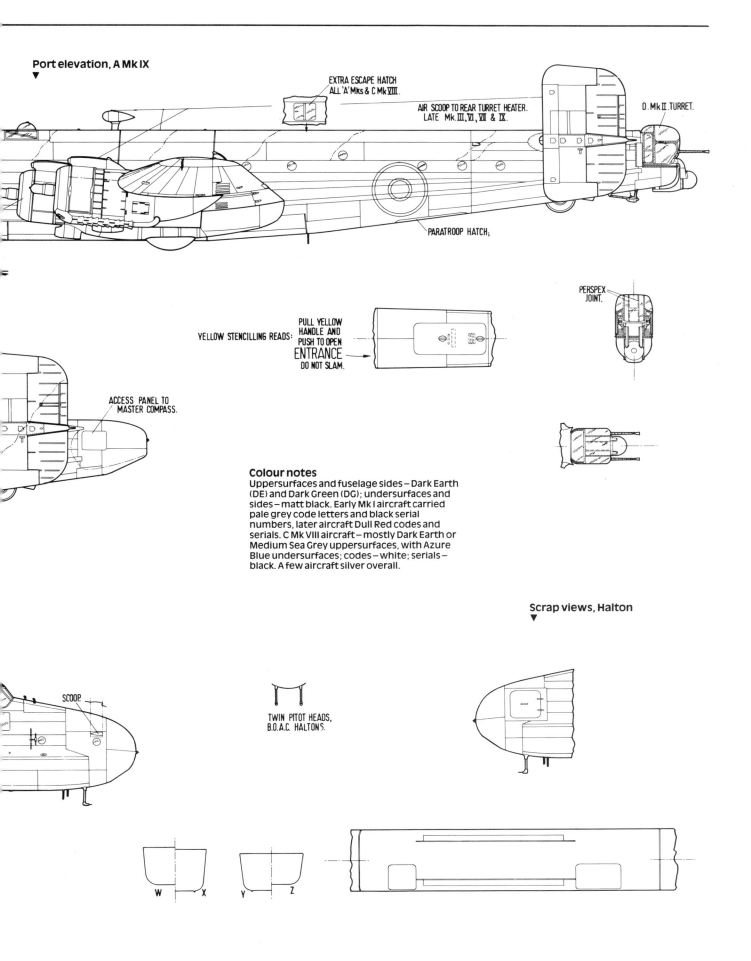

Port elevation, A Mk IX
▼

EXTRA ESCAPE HATCH
ALL 'A' Mks & C Mk VIII.

AIR SCOOP TO REAR TURRET HEATER.
LATE Mk. III, VI, VII & IX.

D. Mk II. TURRET.

PARATROOP HATCH;

PERSPEX JOINT.

ACCESS PANEL TO MASTER COMPASS.

YELLOW STENCILLING READS:
PULL YELLOW HANDLE AND PUSH TO OPEN
ENTRANCE
DO NOT SLAM.

Colour notes
Uppersurfaces and fuselage sides – Dark Earth (DE) and Dark Green (DG); undersurfaces and sides – matt black. Early Mk I aircraft carried pale grey code letters and black serial numbers, later aircraft Dull Red codes and serials. C Mk VIII aircraft – mostly Dark Earth or Medium Sea Grey uppersurfaces, with Azure Blue undersurfaces; codes – white; serials – black. A few aircraft silver overall.

Scrap views, Halton
▼

SCOOP.

TWIN PITOT HEADS,
B.O.A.C. HALTONS.

W   X   Y   Z

Martin B-26A and B Marauder

Country of origin: USA.
Type: Land-based medium bomber.
Dimensions: Wing span 65ft 0in *19.81m*, (B) 71ft 0in *21.64m*; length 56ft 6in *17.22m*; height 21ft 2in *6.45m*; wing area 658 sq ft *61.13m²*.
Weights: Empty 25,300lb *11,474kg*; maximum loaded 38,200lb *17,324kg*.

Powerplant: Two Pratt & Whitney R-2800-39 eighteen-cylinder radial engines each rated at 2000hp, (B) R-2800-43 each at 2000hp.
Performance: Maximum speed 287mph *462kph* at 5000ft *1525m*; service ceiling 19,800ft *6035m*.
Armament: Up to 5800lb *2630kg* of

bombs in fuselage bays, plus five 0.5in machine guns; (B) up to 4000lb *1814kg* of bombs plus up to thirteen 0.5in machine guns.
Service: First flight 25 November 1940; service entry spring 1941.

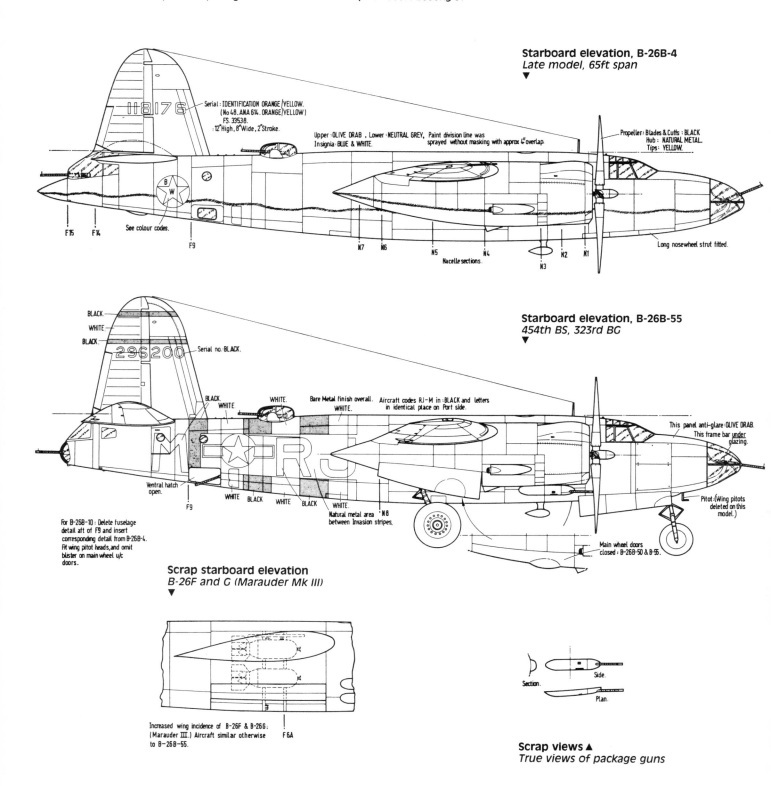

Starboard elevation, B-26B-4
Late model, 65ft span
▼

Serial: IDENTIFICATION ORANGE/YELLOW. (No 48. ANA 614. ORANGE/YELLOW) FS. 33538. 12" High, 8" Wide, 2" Stroke.

Upper: OLIVE DRAB, Lower: NEUTRAL GREY. Paint division line was sprayed without masking with approx 4" overlap. Insignia: BLUE & WHITE.

Propeller: Blades & Cuffs: BLACK. Hub: NATURAL METAL. Tips: YELLOW.

See colour codes.

Long nosewheel strut fitted.

F15 F14 F9 N7 N6 N5 N4 N3 N2 N1
Nacelle sections.

Starboard elevation, B-26B-55
454th BS, 323rd BG
▼

BLACK.
WHITE.
BLACK.
Serial no: BLACK.

296200

BLACK.
WHITE.
WHITE.
WHITE.
Bare Metal finish overall. Aircraft codes RJ-M in BLACK and letters in identical place on Port side.

This panel anti-glare: OLIVE DRAB. This frame bar under glazing.

Ventral hatch open.

F9 WHITE BLACK WHITE BLACK WHITE Natural metal area between Invasion stripes. N8

For B-26B-10: Delete fuselage detail aft of F9 and insert corresponding detail from B-26B-4. Fit wing pitot heads, and omit blister on main wheel u/c doors.

Pitot: (Wing pitots deleted on this model.)

Main wheel doors closed: B-26B-50 & B-55.

Scrap starboard elevation
B-26F and G (Marauder Mk III)
▼

Increased wing incidence of B-26F & B-26G (Marauder III.) Aircraft similar otherwise to B-26B-55.

F6A

Section. Side.
Plan.

Scrap views ▲
True views of package guns

Fuselage cross-sections
▼

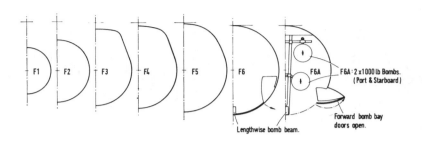

F1 F2 F3 F4 F5 F6 F6A F6A: 2 x 1000 lb Bombs. (Port & Starboard)

Lengthwise bomb beam.

Forward bomb bay doors open.

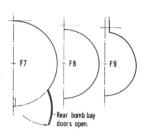

F7 F8 F9

Rear bomb bay doors open.

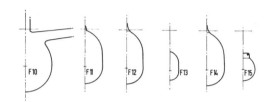

F10 F11 F12 F13 F14 F15

DRAWN BY G R DUVAL
TRACED BY A A P LLOYD

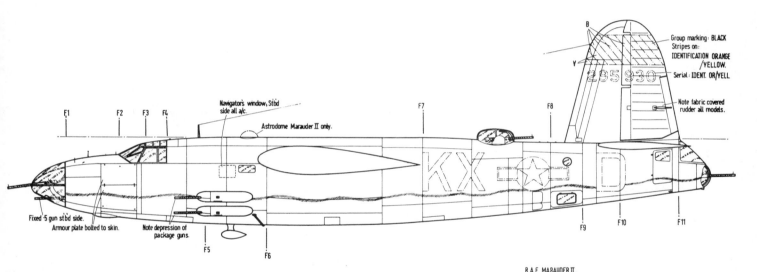

Group marking: BLACK
Stripes on: IDENTIFICATION ORANGE /YELLOW.
Serial: IDENT. OR/YELL.

Note fabric covered rudder all models.

Navigator's window, St'bd side all a/c.

Astrodome Marauder II only.

F1 F2 F3 F4 F7 F8

Fixed ·5 gun st'bd side.
Armour plate bolted to skin.
Note depression of package guns.

F5 F6 F9 F10 F11

▲
Port elevation, B-26B-50
558th BS, 387th BG

Uppersurfaces: OLIVE DRAB. (No 41. ANA.613: FS 34087.)
Lowersurfaces: NEUTRAL GREY. (No 43. ANA 603: From late '43.)
Codeletters: DARK SEA GREY (British paints) Later became SEA GREY: ANA 603. As for undersides from Sept. '43 on camouflaged B-26's.

R.A.F. MARAUDER II.
Basic colour scheme as above. Roundel & Fin flash, also serial, positioned as Marauder I. Aircraft FB 482 Also carried U.S.A.A.F. Serial 135520.
R.A.F. OCEAN GREY, also occasionally used.

Insignia Colour codes.

RED: No 45. ANA 618.
WHITE: No 46. ANA 601. FS 37875.
BLUE: No 47. ANA 605. FS 35044.
IDENT. O/Y: No 48. ANA 614. FS 33538.

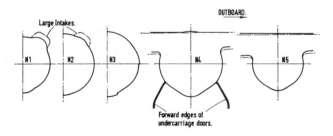

Large Intakes.

OUTBOARD.

N1 N2 N3 N4 N5

Forward edges of undercarriage doors.

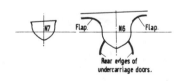

N7 Flap. N6 Flap.

Rear edges of undercarriage doors.

N8

Flap. Flap.

Chain lines show cross-sections for 71ft span wing.

▲ **Nacelle cross-sections**

Scale
0 1 2 3 4 5 6 7 8 ft
0   1   2 m

▲ A USAAF B-26C. This model was identical to the B-10 version
(RAF designation Marauder Mk II).

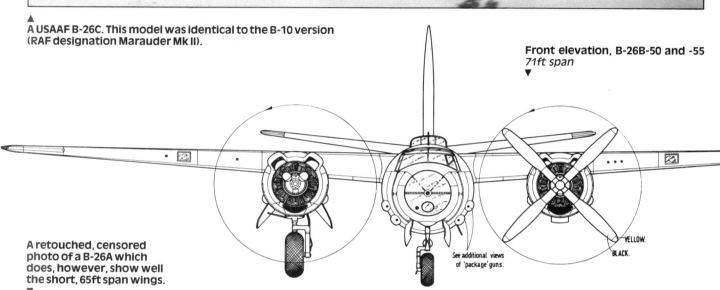

Front elevation, B-26B-50 and -55
71ft span
▼

YELLOW.

BLACK.

See additional views
of 'package' guns.

A retouched, censored
photo of a B-26A which
does, however, show well
the short, 65ft span wings.
▼

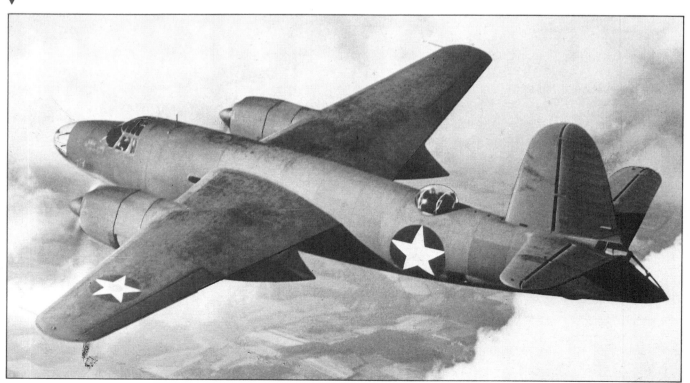

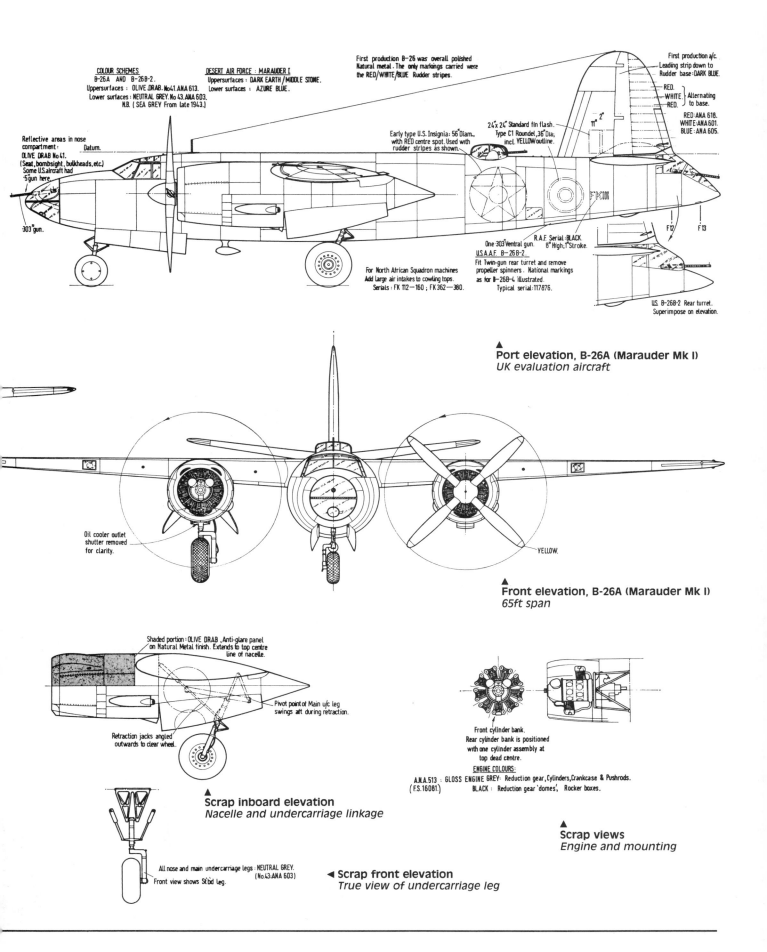

COLOUR SCHEMES
B-26A AND B-26B-2.
Uppersurfaces : OLIVE DRAB. No.41. ANA 613.
Lower surfaces : NEUTRAL GREY. No 43. ANA 603.
N.B. (SEA GREY From late 1943.)

DESERT AIR FORCE : MARAUDER I
Uppersurfaces : DARK EARTH / MIDDLE STONE.
Lower surfaces : AZURE BLUE.

First production B-26 was overall polished
Natural metal. The only markings carried were
the RED/WHITE/BLUE Rudder stripes.

First production a/c.
Leading strip down to
Rudder base: DARK BLUE.

RED.
WHITE } Alternating
RED. } to base.

RED: ANA 618.
WHITE: ANA 601.
BLUE: ANA 605.

Reflective areas in nose
compartment :   Datum.
OLIVE DRAB No 41.
(Seat, bombsight, bulkheads, etc.)
Some U.S. aircraft had
·5 gun here.

·303 gun.

Early type U.S. Insignia: 56" Diam.,
with RED centre spot. Used with
rudder stripes as shown.

24" x 24" Standard fin flash.
Type C1 Roundel, 36" Dia;
incl. YELLOW outline.

11"

2"

FK30□

One ·303 Ventral gun.

R.A.F. Serial: BLACK.
8" High, 1" Stroke.

F12   F13

For North African Squadron machines
Add large air intakes to cowling tops.
Serials : FK 112—160 ; FK 362—380.

U.S.A.A.F. B-26B-2.
Fit Twin-gun rear turret and remove
propeller spinners. National markings
as for B-26B-4 illustrated.
Typical serial: 117876.

U.S. B-26B-2. Rear turret.
Superimpose on elevation.

▲ **Port elevation, B-26A (Marauder Mk I)**
UK evaluation aircraft

Oil cooler outlet
shutter removed
for clarity.

YELLOW.

▲ **Front elevation, B-26A (Marauder Mk I)**
65ft span

Shaded portion : OLIVE DRAB , Anti-glare panel
on Natural Metal finish. Extends to top centre
line of nacelle.

Pivot point of Main u/c leg
swings aft during retraction.

Retraction jacks angled
outwards to clear wheel.

▲ **Scrap inboard elevation**
Nacelle and undercarriage linkage

Front cylinder bank.
Rear cylinder bank is positioned
with one cylinder assembly at
top dead centre.

ENGINE COLOURS:
A.N.A.513 : GLOSS ENGINE GREY: Reduction gear, Cylinders, Crankcase & Pushrods.
(F.S.16081.)
BLACK : Reduction gear 'domes', Rocker boxes.

▲ **Scrap views**
Engine and mounting

All nose and main undercarriage legs : NEUTRAL GREY.
(No.43: ANA 603)
Front view shows St'bd leg.

◀ **Scrap front elevation**
True view of undercarriage leg

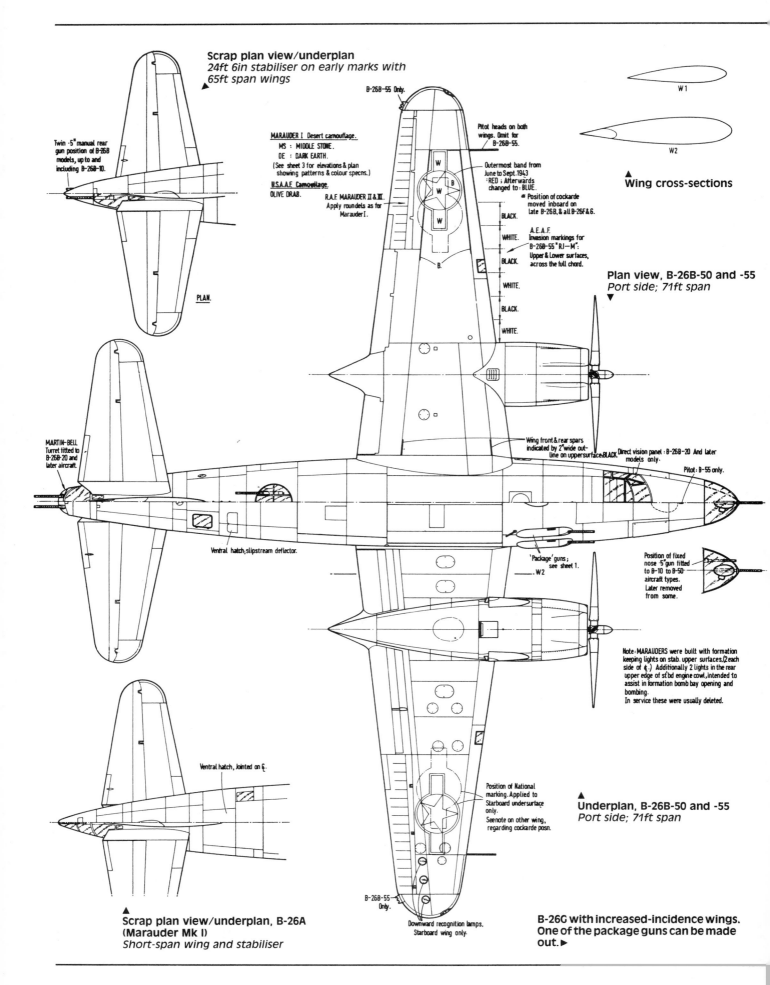

Scrap plan view/underplan
24ft 6in stabiliser on early marks with 65ft span wings ▲

Twin ·5" manual rear gun position of B-26B models, up to and including B-26B-10.

PLAN.

B-26B-55 Only.

MARAUDER I Desert camouflage.
MS : MIDDLE STONE.
DE : DARK EARTH.
(See sheet 3 for elevations & plan showing patterns & colour specns.)
U.S.A.A.F. Camouflage.
OLIVE DRAB.
R.A.F. MARAUDER II & III. Apply roundels as for Marauder I.

Pitot heads on both wings. Omit for B-26B-55.

Outermost band from June to Sept.1943 : RED; Afterwards changed to: BLUE.

✱ Position of cockarde moved inboard on late B-26B, & all B-26F&G.

A.E.A.F. Invasion markings for B-26B-55 "RJ—M": Upper & Lower surfaces, across the full chord.

BLACK.
WHITE.
BLACK.
WHITE.
BLACK.
WHITE.

W1

W2

▲ **Wing cross-sections**

Plan view, B-26B-50 and -55
Port side; 71ft span ▼

MARTIN-BELL Turret fitted to B-26B-20 and later aircraft.

Wing front & rear spars indicated by 2"wide outline on upper surface.BLACK.

Direct vision panel : B-26B-20 And later models only.

Pitot : B-55 only.

Ventral hatch, slipstream deflector.

'Package' guns ; see sheet 1.

W2

Position of fixed nose ·5"gun fitted to B-10 to B-50 aircraft types. Later removed from some.

Note: MARAUDERS were built with formation keeping lights on stab. upper surfaces.(2 each side of ₵.) Additionally 2 lights in the rear upper edge of st'bd engine cowl, intended to assist in formation bomb bay opening and bombing.
In service these were usually deleted.

Ventral hatch, Jointed on ₵.

Position of National marking. Applied to Starboard undersurface only.
See note on other wing, regarding cockarde posn.

Underplan, B-26B-50 and -55
Port side; 71ft span ▲

B-26B-55 Only.

Downward recognition lamps. Starboard wing only.

▲ **Scrap plan view/underplan, B-26A (Marauder Mk I)**
Short-span wing and stabiliser

B-26G with increased-incidence wings. One of the package guns can be made out. ▶

Marauder Mk IA (B-26B) of No 14 Squadron in RAF desert camouflage. The legend on the nose reads 'Dominion Revenge'. ▶

Scale
0 1 2 3 4 5 6 7 8 ft
0   1   2 m

Scrap underplan
Port side; 65ft span
▼

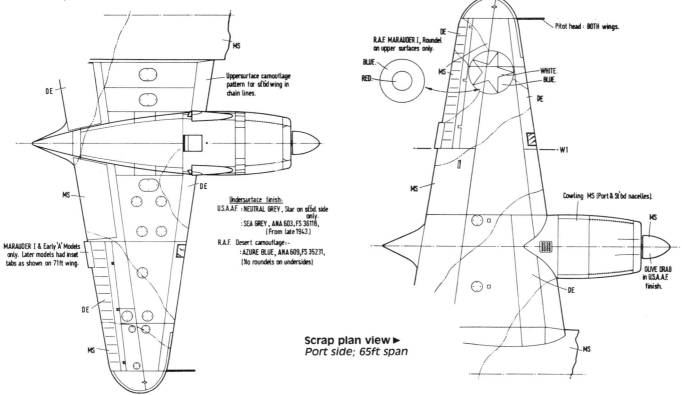

MS

Uppersurface camouflage pattern for st'bd wing in chain lines.

DE

MS

MARAUDER I & Early 'A' Models only. Later models had inset tabs as shown on 71ft wing.

DE

MS

DE

Undersurface finish:
U.S.A.A.F. : NEUTRAL GREY, Star on st'bd. side only.
: SEA GREY, ANA 603, FS 36118, (From late 1943.)

R.A.F. Desert camouflage :-
: AZURE BLUE, ANA 609, FS 35231, (No roundels on undersides)

Pitot head : BOTH wings.

R.A.F. MARAUDER I, Roundel on upper surfaces only.

BLUE
RED

DE
MS

WHITE.
BLUE.
DE

W1

MS

Cowling MS (Port & St'bd nacelles).

MS

DE

OLIVE DRAB in U.S.A.A.F. finish.

Scrap plan view ▶
Port side; 65ft span

MS

295743

Junkers Ju 87D and G 'Stuka'

Country of origin: Germany.
Type: Two-seat, land-based dive bomber and ground attack aircraft.
Dimensions: Wing span 45ft 3½in *13.80m*; length 37ft 8¾in *11.50m*; height 12ft 9¼in *3.89m*; wing area 343.37 sq ft *31.9m²*.
Weights: (D) Empty equipped 8600lb *3900kg*; normal loaded 12,877lb *5840kg*;

maximum 14,553lb *6600kg*.
Powerplant: One Junkers Jumo 211J-1 twelve-cylinder, liquid-cooled piston engine rated at 1400hp.
Performance: Maximum speed 255mph *410kph*; time to 16,400ft *5000m*, 19.8min; service ceiling 23,950ft *7300m*; range (normal) 509 miles *820km*.
Armament: Up to 3970lb *1800kg* of

bombs on fuselage cradle and wing racks plus two fixed 7.9mm MG 17 machine guns and two flexibly mounted 7.9mm MG 81 machine guns, (G, optional) two fixed 37mm BK cannon beneath wings.
Service: First flight (Ju 87 V1) spring 1935, (D) early 1941, (G) summer 1942; service entry (D) spring 1941.

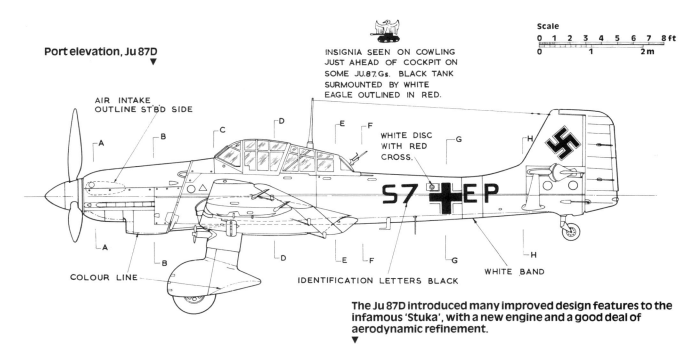

Port elevation, Ju 87D

AIR INTAKE OUTLINE ST'BD SIDE

INSIGNIA SEEN ON COWLING JUST AHEAD OF COCKPIT ON SOME JU.87.Gs. BLACK TANK SURMOUNTED BY WHITE EAGLE OUTLINED IN RED.

Scale

WHITE DISC WITH RED CROSS.

COLOUR LINE

IDENTIFICATION LETTERS BLACK

WHITE BAND

The Ju 87D introduced many improved design features to the infamous 'Stuka', with a new engine and a good deal of aerodynamic refinement.

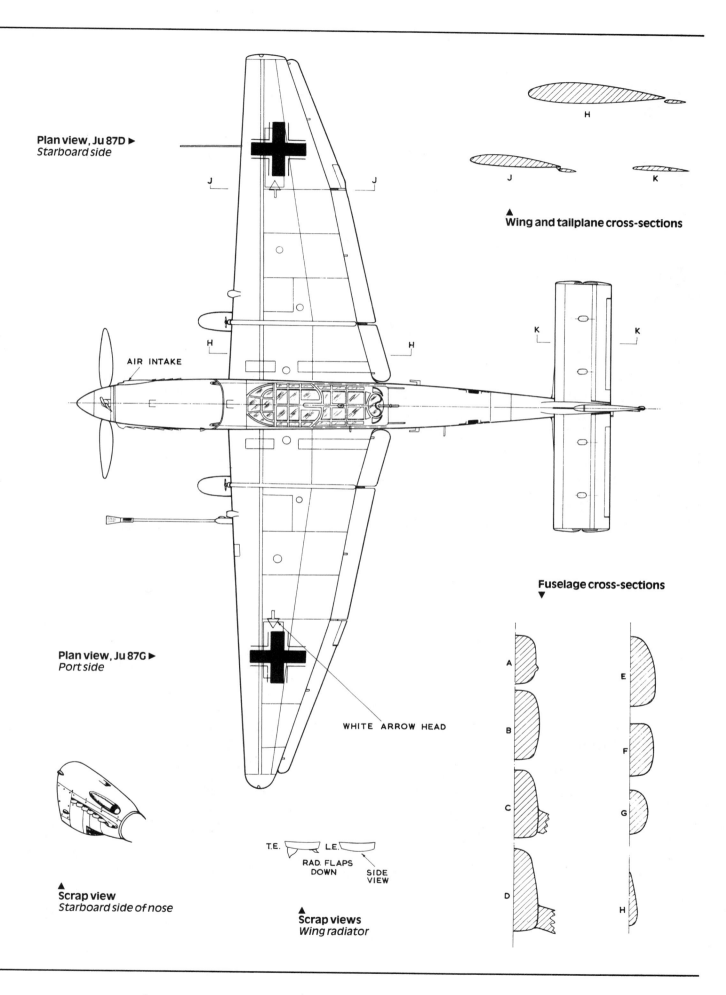

Plan view, Ju 87D ▶
Starboard side

AIR INTAKE

J   J

H   H

Plan view, Ju 87G ▶
Port side

WHITE ARROW HEAD

▲
Scrap view
Starboard side of nose

T.E. ⌐‾⌐ L.E. ⌐‾⌐
RAD. FLAPS   SIDE
DOWN   VIEW

▲
Scrap views
Wing radiator

▲
Wing and tailplane cross-sections

H

J   K

K   K

Fuselage cross-sections
▼

A   E

B   F

C   G

D   H

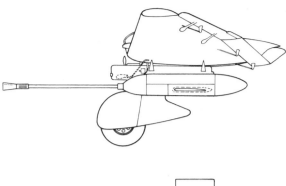

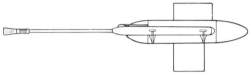

▲
Scrap plan view and port elevation,
Ju 87G
*Showing 37mm gun detail (port and
starboard guns not handed)*

◄ Business end of the port 37mm cannon of a Ju 87G.
Considerable success attended the deployment of this tank-
busting version of the 'Stuka', especially on the Russian
Front.

The Ju 87G was a converted D-5, and the cannon pods could
readily be removed in favour of bomb racks in the field.
▼

DRAWN BY J D McHARD

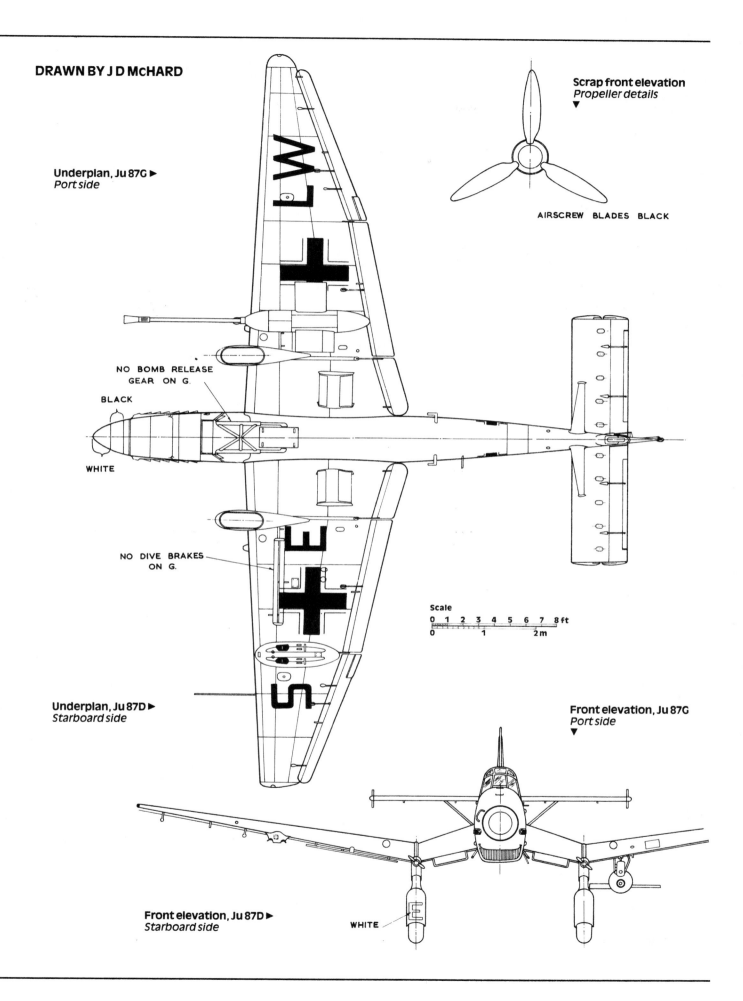

Scrap front elevation
Propeller details
▼

AIRSCREW BLADES BLACK

Underplan, Ju 87G ►
Port side

NO BOMB RELEASE
GEAR ON G.

BLACK

WHITE

NO DIVE BRAKES
ON G.

Underplan, Ju 87D ►
Starboard side

Scale
0 1 2 3 4 5 6 7 8 ft
0   1   2 m

Front elevation, Ju 87G
Port side
▼

Front elevation, Ju 87D ►
Starboard side

WHITE

Avro Lancaster B Mks I and III

Country of origin: Great Britain.
Type: Land-based heavy bomber.
Dimensions: Wing span 102ft 0in *31.09m*; length 69ft 4in *21.13m*; height 20ft 0in *6.10m*; wing area 1297 sq ft *120.49m²*.
Weights: Empty 37,000lb *16,780kg*; normal loaded 68,000lb *20,727kg*.
Powerplant: Four Rolls-Royce Merlin XX

V12, liquid-cooled piston engines each rated at 1280hp, (Mk III) Packard Merlin 28 rated at 1280hp.
Performance: Maximum speed 275mph *442kph*; time to 20,000ft *6100m*, 42min; service ceiling (maximum bomb load) 20,000ft; range 3000 miles *4830km*.
Armament: Up to 18,000lb *8163kg* of

bombs in fuselage bay, plus eight or ten turret-mounted 0.303in Browning machine guns.
Service: First flight (Mk I prototype) 9 January 1941, (production Mk I) 31 October 1941; service entry (Mk I) December 1941.

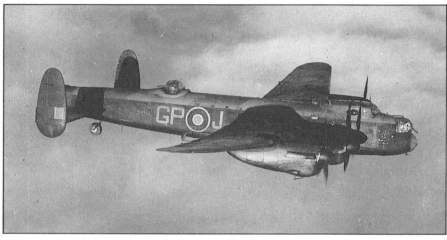

Scale

▲
Developed from the failed twin-engined Manchester, the Lancaster proved to be the RAF's outstanding heavy bomber of the war.

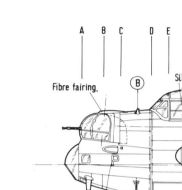

Fibre fairing.

Yellow.

◀ **Fuselage cross-sections**
Special aircraft

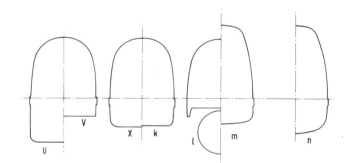

SPECIAL B.Mk1.
Camouflaged as other aircraft.
Serial No. Unknown for YZ-C.
Modified aircraft in 617 Sqdn.
were PD 112, PD 317. —;
PD 139 was YZ-W &
PD 114 was YZ-B.

Fuselage sides, Interior of wing at flap area, Bomb bay & Undercarriage compartments: Matt Black, (Night - Spec. DTD 314), To this line.

YZ-J Finished in Standard Day camouflage over fuse. sides. & Lt.Grey undersides.

Modified to carry the 22,000lb 'Grand Slam' bomb.

Open rear to glazing.

1" Line.

Yellow.
Blue.
White
Red.

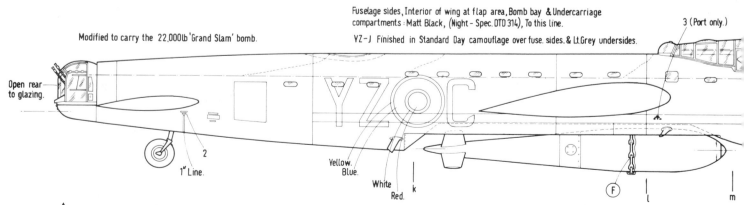

3 (Port only.)

▲
Starboard elevation, B Mk I (Special)
Wing and tailplane omitted to show detail

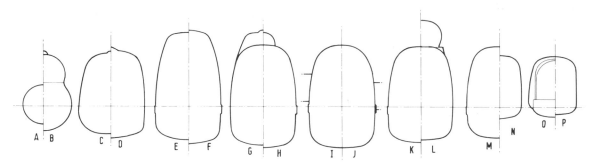

▲ Fuselage cross-sections
Standard aircraft

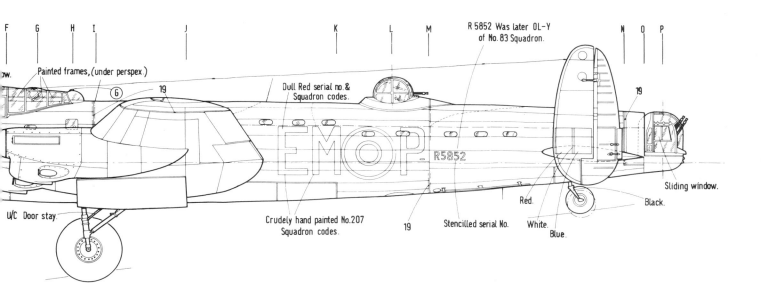

F G H I   J   K   L   M   R 5852 Was later OL-Y   N   O   P
                                                         of No. 83 Squadron.

Painted frames, (under perspex.)

⑥   19

Dull Red serial no. &
Squadron codes.

19

Sliding window.

U/C Door stay.

Crudely hand painted No.207   Red.   Black.
Squadron codes.   Stencilled serial No.   White.
                           19   Blue.

▲ Port elevation, B Mk I

**A photo taken during the massed low-level raid on Le Creusot
by 94 Lancasters on 17 October 1942.**
▼

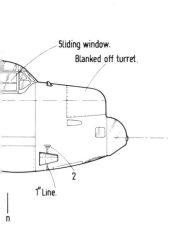

Sliding window.
Blanked off turret.

2

1" Line.

n

Nacelle cross-sections
▼

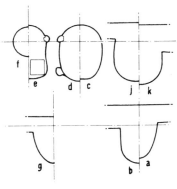

Wing and tail cross-sections
▼

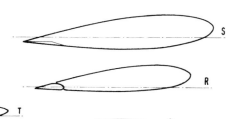

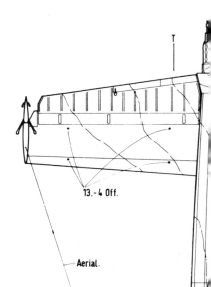

13. - 4 Off.

Aerial.

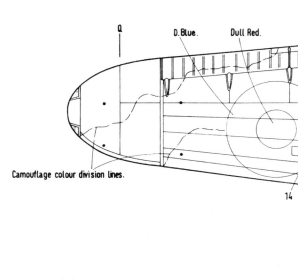

D. Blue. Dull Red.

Camouflage colour division lines.

14

$1\frac{1}{2}''$ Black lines.

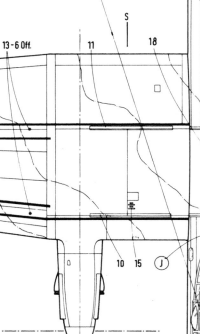

13 - 6 Off.

Spinners & Propellers : Black.
Propeller tips : Yellow.

Scrap starboard elevation ▼
Port inner nacelle

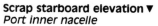

This panel Port side only.

Colour line.

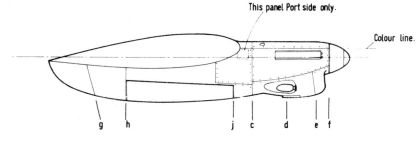

▲
Plan view, B Mk I
Starboard side

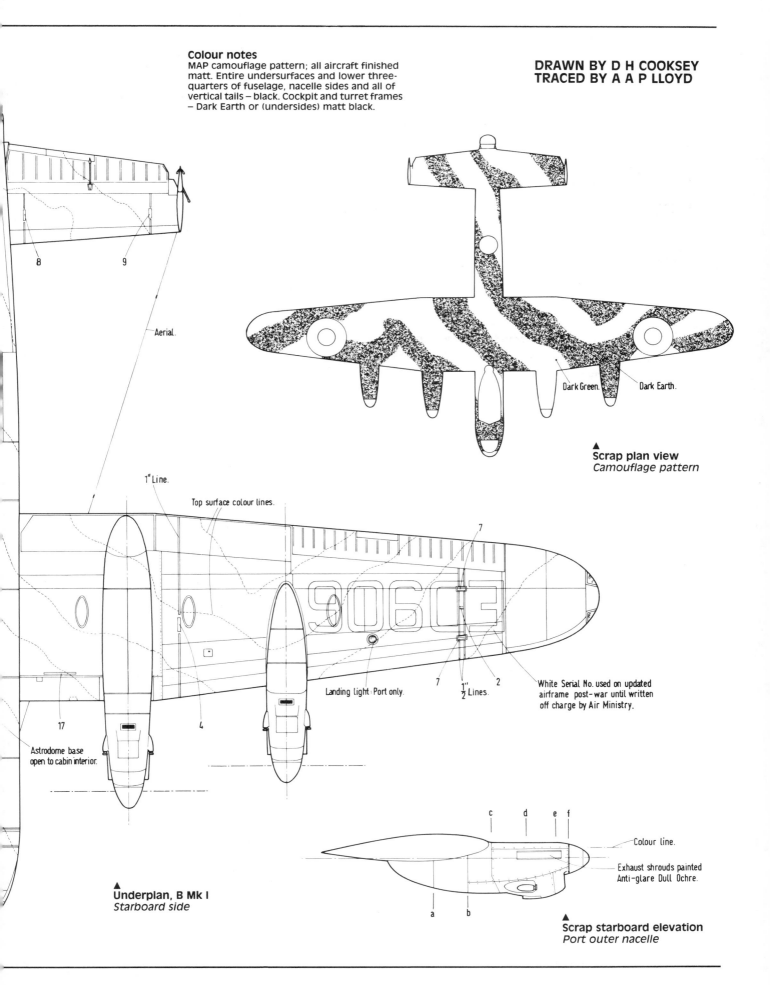

Colour notes

MAP camouflage pattern; all aircraft finished matt. Entire undersurfaces and lower three-quarters of fuselage, nacelle sides and all of vertical tails – black. Cockpit and turret frames – Dark Earth or (undersides) matt black.

DRAWN BY D H COOKSEY
TRACED BY A A P LLOYD

8   9

Aerial.

Dark Green.   Dark Earth.

▲ **Scrap plan view**
Camouflage pattern

1″ Line.

Top surface colour lines.

7

9060

7   2

7   ½″ Lines.

Landing light - Port only.

17

4

White Serial No. used on updated airframe post-war until written off charge by Air Ministry.

Astrodome base open to cabin interior.

▲ **Underplan, B Mk I**
Starboard side

c   d   e   f

Colour line.

Exhaust shrouds painted Anti-glare Dull Ochre.

a   b

▲ **Scrap starboard elevation**
Port outer nacelle

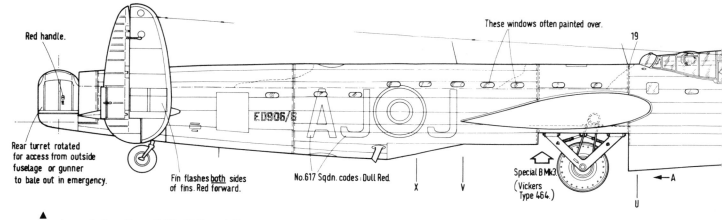

Red handle.

These windows often painted over.

19

Rear turret rotated for access from outside fuselage or gunner to bale out in emergency.

Fin flashes both sides of fins. Red forward.

ED906/6 AJ J

No.617 Sqdn. codes: Dull Red.

X   V

Special B Mk3
(Vickers Type 464.)

A

U

▲ **Starboard elevation, B Mk III (Special)**

Scrap views
Undercarriage geometry (enlarged)
▼

Wingspar box.

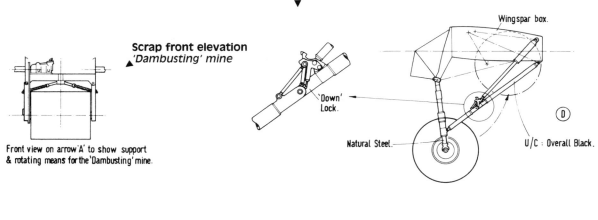

Scrap front elevation
'Dambusting' mine
▲

'Down' Lock.

Natural Steel.

U/C : Overall Black.

Ⓓ

Front view on arrow 'A' to show support & rotating means for the 'Dambusting' mine.

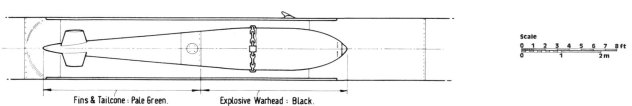

Scale
0 1 2 3 4 5 6 7 8 ft
0   1   2 m

Fins & Tailcone : Pale Green.   Explosive Warhead : Black.

Shows modified Bomb bay area with 22,000lb Grand Slam installed.

▼**Scrap underplan, B Mk I (Special)**

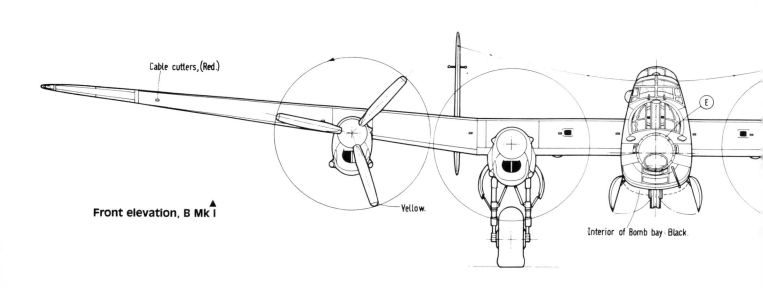

Cable cutters, (Red.)

E

Front elevation, B Mk I
▲

Yellow.

Interior of Bomb bay : Black.

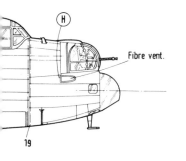

H

Fibre vent.

19

STENCILLING : Dull Red.

2. "TRESTLE HERE."
3. "C G ORIGIN." } 1" Letters.

4. "RIB 20."
5. "PULL."
6. "FIRST AID"
7. "SPAR."
8. "RIB 2."
9. "RIB 12." } 1½" Letters.

10. "WALK AFT OF THIS LINE."
11. "WALK FORWARD OF THIS LINE." } 3" Letters.
12. "WALK HERE."

13. 1½" DIA. BLACK DOTS.

14. "TANK NO.3.   15. "TANK NO.2.   16. "TANK NO.1.
FUEL   **FUEL**   **FUEL**
100 OCTANE   100 OCTANE   100 OCTANE
ONLY. "   ONLY. "   ONLY. " } Black.

17. "-FIT JACKING PADS HERE-"   Dull Red.

18. " DINGHY RELEASE
       PULL HARD   Black.
    EMERGENCY ONLY. "

19. Doped fabric sealing strip over manufacturing
                                   transport joints.

▲
L7532, a B Mk I, disarmed and with bomb doors open, lies derelict at the end of the war.

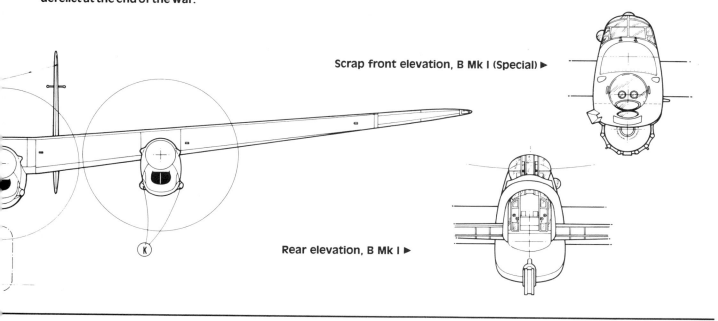

K

Scrap front elevation, B Mk I (Special) ▶

Rear elevation, B Mk I ▶

Avro Lancaster B.Mk. I sketch page

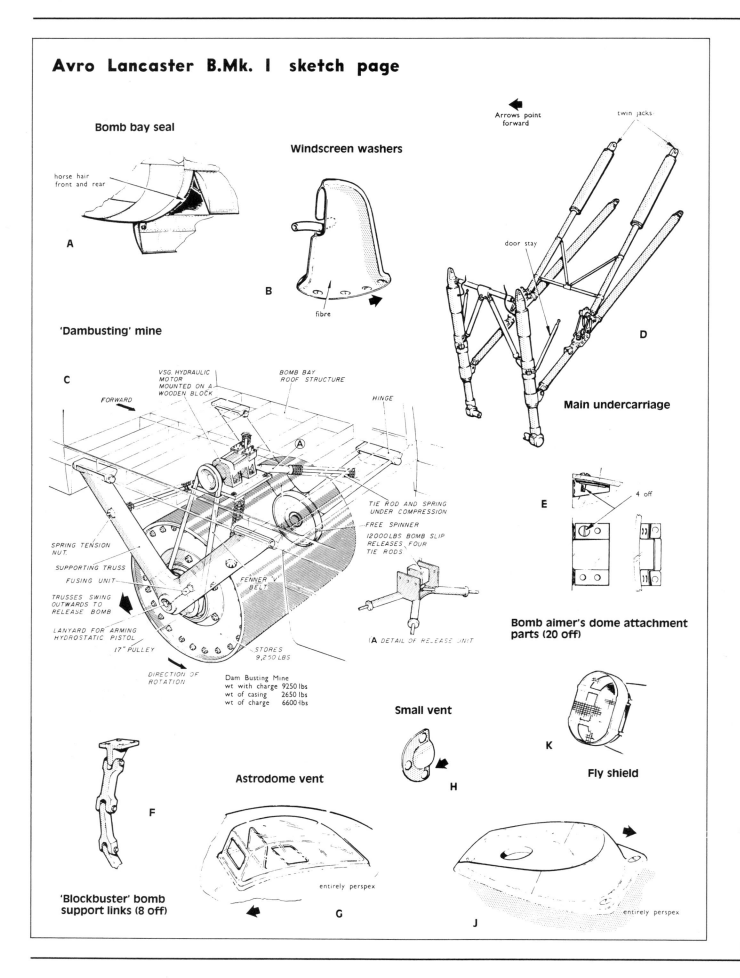

Bomb bay seal

horse hair
front and rear

A

Windscreen washers

B

fibre

Arrows point
forward

twin jacks

door stay

D

Main undercarriage

'Dambusting' mine

C

FORWARD

VSG. HYDRAULIC
MOTOR
MOUNTED ON A
WOODEN BLOCK

BOMB BAY
ROOF STRUCTURE

HINGE

Ⓐ

TIE ROD AND SPRING
UNDER COMPRESSION

FREE SPINNER

12000 LBS BOMB SLIP
RELEASES FOUR
TIE RODS

SPRING TENSION
NUT.

SUPPORTING TRUSS

FUSING UNIT

TRUSSES SWING
OUTWARDS TO
RELEASE BOMB

LANYARD FOR ARMING
HYDROSTATIC PISTOL

17" PULLEY

FENNER 'V'
BELT

STORES
9,250 LBS

DIRECTION OF
ROTATION

Dam Busting Mine
wt with charge 9250 lbs
wt of casing 2650 lbs
wt of charge 6600 lbs

Ⓐ DETAIL OF RELEASE UNIT

E

4 off

**Bomb aimer's dome attachment
parts (20 off)**

K

Fly shield

Small vent

H

Astrodome vent

entirely perspex

G

F

**'Blockbuster' bomb
support links (8 off)**

entirely perspex

J

78

▲
Some 300 Lancaster B Mk IIs, fitted with Hercules radials, were built by Armstrong-Whitworth. DS689 'OW-S' served with No 426 Squadron RCAF.

B.Is in peacetime livery. These are Lancasters from No 35 Squadron, just prior to a goodwill tour of the USA in July 1946.
▼

Ilyushin Il-2 'Stormovik'

Country of origin: USSR.
Type: Two-seat, land-based ground attack bomber.
Dimensions: Wing span 47ft 11in *14.60m*; length 38ft 1in *11.60m*; wing area 414.4 sq ft *38.5m²*.
Weights: Empty 9978lb *4525kg*; normal loaded 12,950lb *5873kg*; maximum 14,024lb *6360kg*.

Powerplant: One Mikulin AM-38F V12, liquid-cooled piston engine rated at 1750 or (later) 1770hp.
Performance: Maximum speed 251mph *404kph* at 4920ft *1500m*; time to 16,400ft *5000m*, 12min; service ceiling 11,500ft *3500m*; range 475 miles *765km*.
Armament: Eight 82mm RS82 or 132mm RS132 rocket projectiles or up to 1323lb

600kg of bombs on wing racks, plus two fixed 23mm VYa cannon, two fixed 7.6mm ShKas machine guns and one flexibly mounted 12.7mm BS machine gun.
Service: First flight (BSh-2 prototype) late 1939, (Il-2) July 1942; service entry (Il-2) autumn 1942.

Port elevation ▼

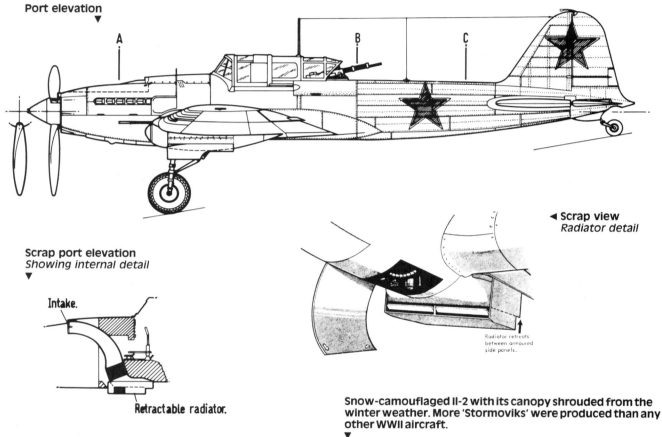

◄ Scrap view
Radiator detail

Radiator retreats between armoured side panels.

Scrap port elevation
Showing internal detail ▼

Intake.

Retractable radiator.

Snow-camouflaged Il-2 with its canopy shrouded from the winter weather. More 'Stormoviks' were produced than any other WWII aircraft.
▼

▲
Chocks away for an Il-2 in more clement conditions. Notice the stars on the undercarriage fairings.

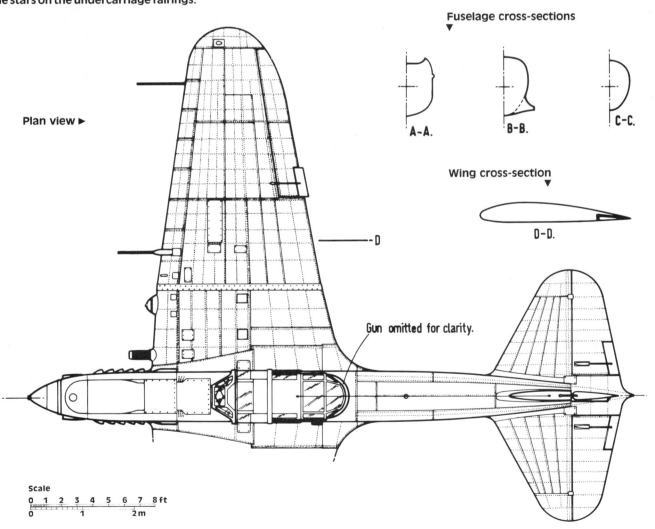

Fuselage cross-sections
▼

A–A. B-B. C-C.

Plan view ►

Wing cross-section
▼

D–D.

— D

Gun omitted for clarity.

Scale

0 1 2 3 4 5 6 7 8 ft

0   1   2 m

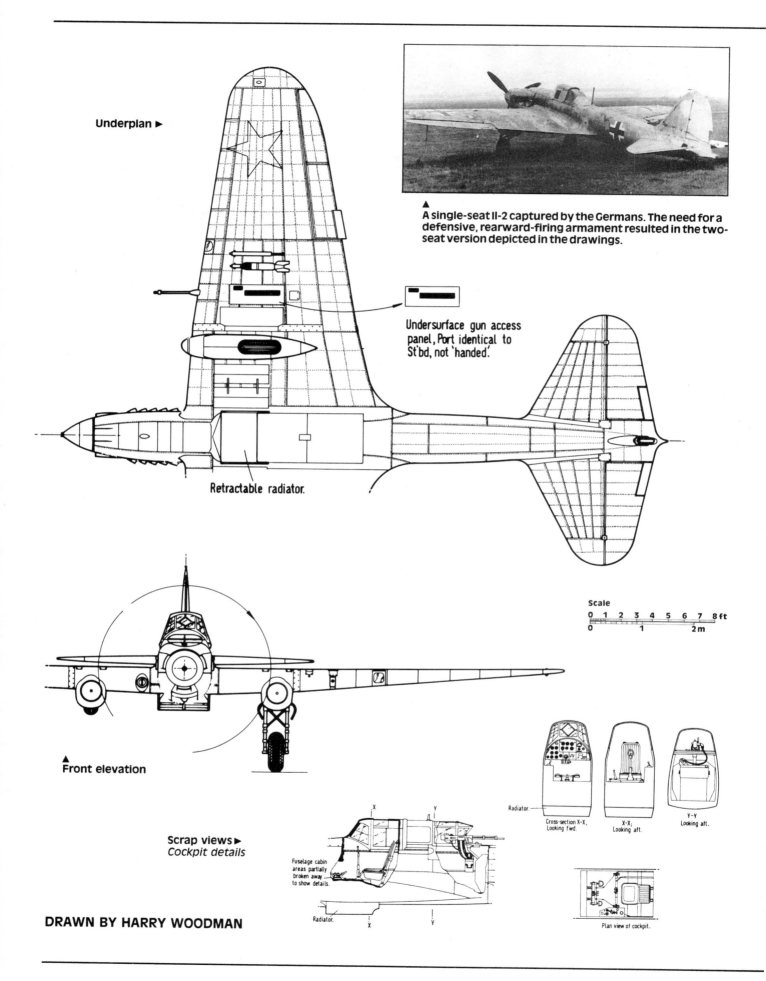

Underplan ▶

A single-seat Il-2 captured by the Germans. The need for a defensive, rearward-firing armament resulted in the two-seat version depicted in the drawings.

Undersurface gun access panel, Port identical to St'bd, not 'handed'.

Retractable radiator.

Scale

0 1 2 3 4 5 6 7 8 ft
0   1   2 m

▲ **Front elevation**

Scrap views ▶
Cockpit details

Fuselage cabin areas partially broken away to show details.

Radiator.

Radiator.

Cross-section X-X, Looking fwd.

X-X, Looking aft.

Y-Y Looking aft.

Plan view of cockpit.

DRAWN BY HARRY WOODMAN

Scrap views
12.7mm BS machine gun
▼

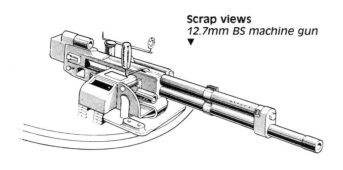

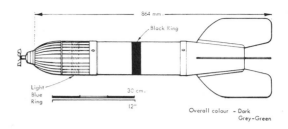

864 mm

Black Ring

Light
Blue
Ring

30 cm.

12"

Overall colour - Dark
Grey-Green

▲
Scrap view
RS132 rocket projectile

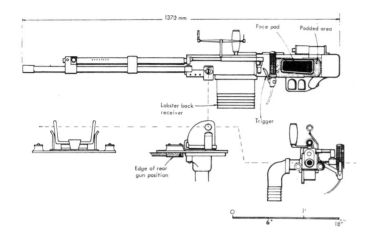

1370 mm

Face pad

Padded area

Lobster back
receiver

Trigger

Edge of rear
gun position

O   1'

6"   18"

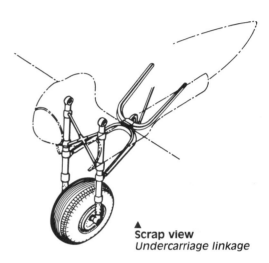

▲
Scrap view
Undercarriage linkage

Known to the Russians as 'The Flying Tank', the Il-2 proved its worth, being both well armed and well armoured for the ground attack role.
▼

Junkers Ju 188E-1

Country of origin: Germany.
Type: Four-seat, land-based medium bomber.
Dimensions: Wing span 72ft 2in *22.0m*; length 49ft 0½in *14.95m*; height 14ft 7in *4.45m*; wing area 602.78 sq ft *56.0m²*.
Weights: Empty equipped 21,741lb *9860kg*; normal loaded 31,983lb *14,505kg*.

Powerplant: Two BMW 801D-2 fourteen-cylinder radial engines each rated at 1700hp.
Performance: Maximum speed 311mph *500kph* at 19,700ft *6000m*; time to 19,700ft, 17.6min; service ceiling 30,675ft *9350m*; range 1210 miles *1950km*.
Armament: Up to 6615lb *3000kg* of

bombs, plus one flexibly mounted 20mm MG 151 cannon, one turret-mounted and one flexibly mounted 13mm MG 131 machine gun and one flexibly mounted 7.9mm MG 81 machine gun.
Service: First flight (Ju 188 V1) late 1942; service entry May 1943.

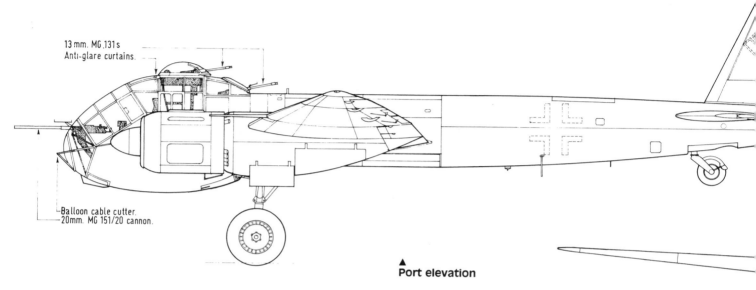

13 mm. MG.131s
Anti-glare curtains.

Balloon cable cutter.
20mm. MG 151/20 cannon.

▲ **Port elevation**

Scrap starboard elevation
▼

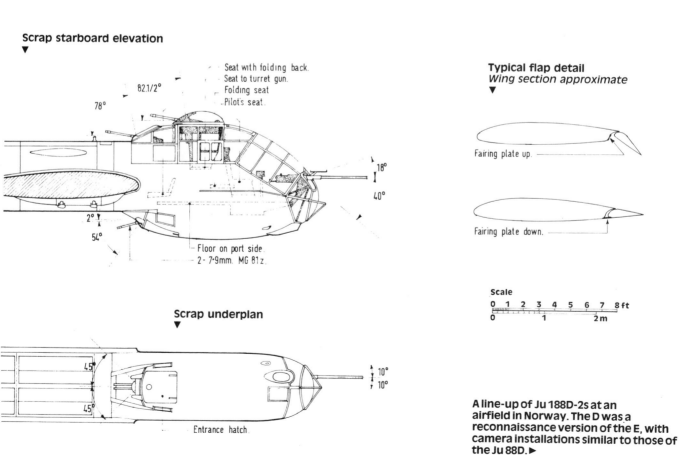

82.1/2°

78°

Seat with folding back.
Seat to turret gun.
Folding seat.
Pilot's seat.

18°

40°

2°

54°

Floor on port side.
2 - 7·9mm. MG 81 z.

Scrap underplan
▼

45°

45°

10°
10°

Entrance hatch.

Typical flap detail
Wing section approximate
▼

Fairing plate up.

Fairing plate down.

Scale

0 1 2 3 4 5 6 7 8 ft
0 1 2 m

A line-up of Ju 188D-2s at an airfield in Norway. The D was a reconnaissance version of the E, with camera installations similar to those of the Ju 88D. ▶

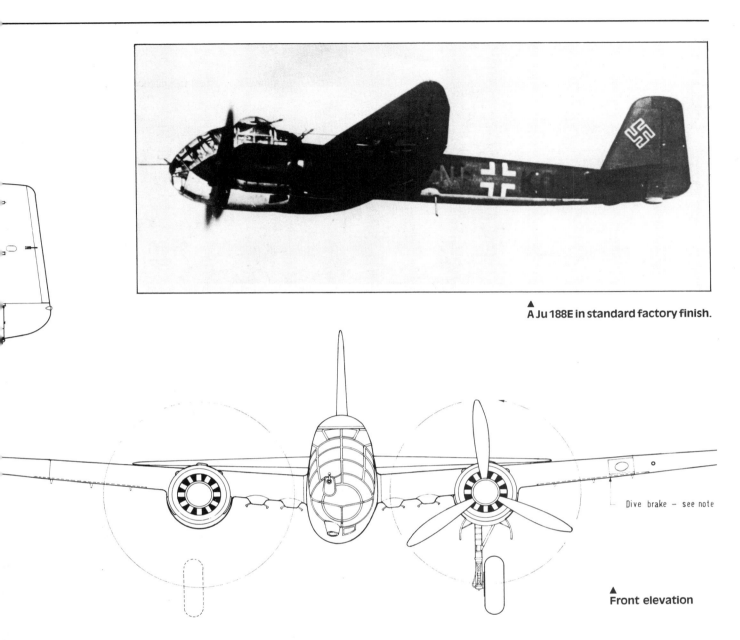

▲ A Ju 188E in standard factory finish.

Dive brake – see note

▲ Front elevation

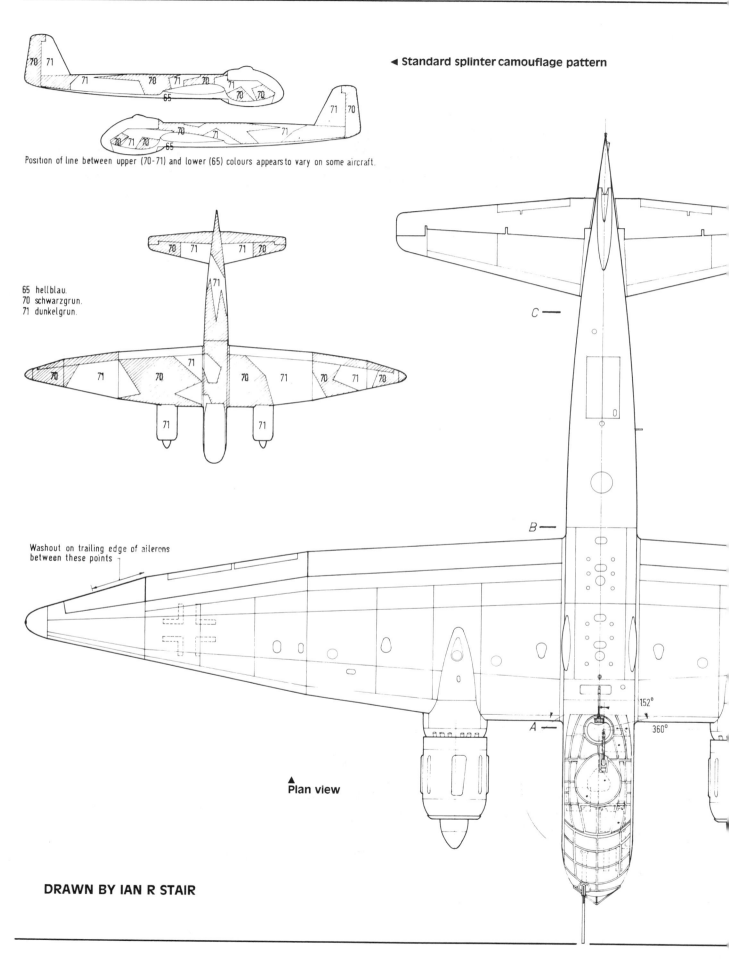

◄ **Standard splinter camouflage pattern**

Position of line between upper (70-71) and lower (65) colours appears to vary on some aircraft.

65 hellblau.
70 schwarzgrun.
71 dunkelgrun.

Washout on trailing edge of ailerons
between these points

152°

360°

▲ **Plan view**

DRAWN BY IAN R STAIR

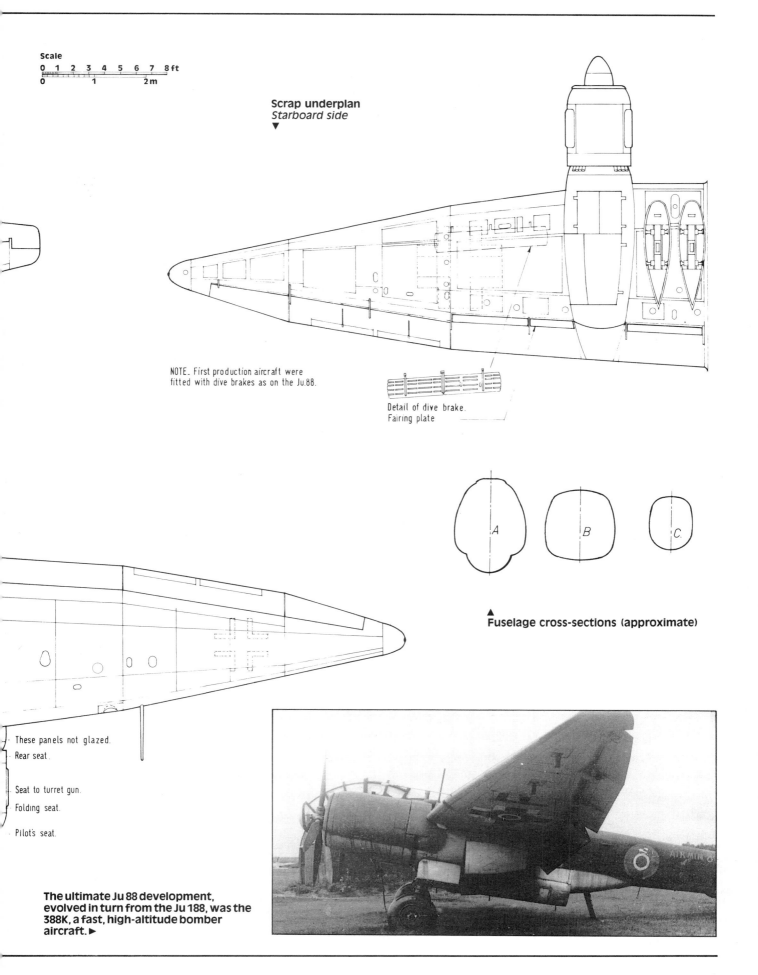

Scale

0 1 2 3 4 5 6 7 8 ft

0 1 2m

Scrap underplan
Starboard side
▼

NOTE. First production aircraft were
fitted with dive brakes as on the Ju.88.

Detail of dive brake.
Fairing plate

A   *B*   *C.*

▲ **Fuselage cross-sections (approximate)**

- These panels not glazed.
- Rear seat.

- Seat to turret gun.
- Folding seat.

- Pilot's seat.

**The ultimate Ju 88 development,
evolved in turn from the Ju 188, was the
388K, a fast, high-altitude bomber
aircraft.** ►

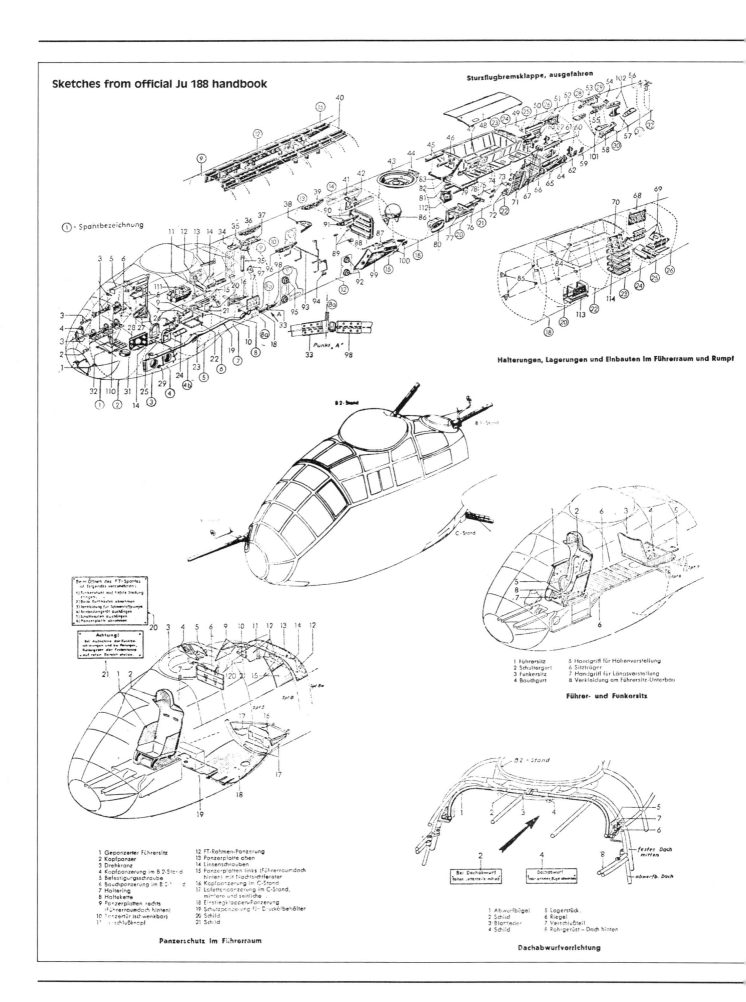

Sketches from official Ju 188 handbook

Sturzflugbremsklappe, ausgefahren

① = Spantbezeichnung

Halterungen, Lagerungen und Einbauten im Führerraum und Rumpf

B 2-Stand

B 1-Stand

C-Stand

Führer- und Funkersitz

1 Führersitz
2 Schultergurt
3 Funkersitz
4 Bauchgurt
5 Handgriff für Höhenverstellung
6 Sitzträger
7 Handgriff für Längsverstellung
8 Verkleidung am Führersitz-Unterbau

Panzerschutz im Führerraum

1 Gepanzerter Führersitz
2 Kopfpanzer
3 Drehkranz
4 Kopfpanzerung im B 2-Stand
5 Befestigungsschraube
6 Bauchpanzerung im B 2-Stand
7 Haltering
8 Haltekette
9 Panzerplatten rechts (Führerraumdach hinten)
10 Panzertür (schwenkbar)
11 Verschlußknopf
12 FT-Rahmen-Panzerung
13 Panzerplatte oben
14 Linsenschrauben
15 Panzerplatten links (Führerraumdach hinten) mit Nachtsichtfenster
16 Kopfpanzerung im C-Stand
17 Lafettenpanzerung im C-Stand, mittlere und seitliche
18 Einstiegklappen-Panzerung
19 Schutzpanzerung für Drucköölbehälter
20 Schild
21 Schild

Dachabwurfvorrichtung

1 Abwurfbügel
2 Schild
3 Blattfeder
4 Schild
5 Lagerstück
6 Riegel
7 Verschlußteil
8 Rohrgerüst – Dach hinten

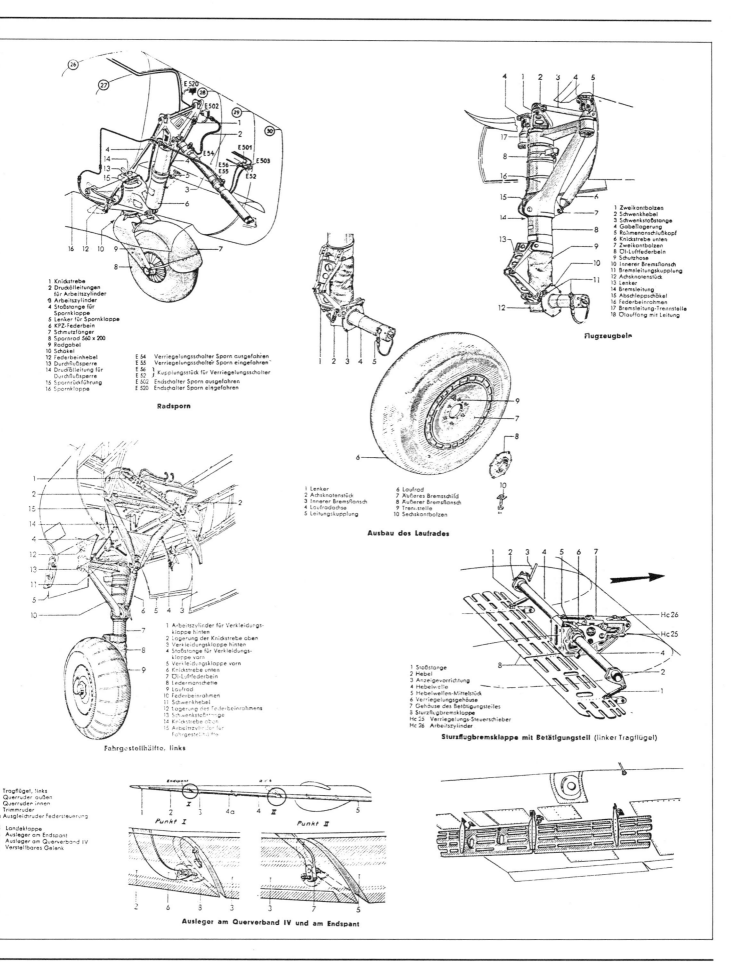

Radsporn

1 Knickstrebe
2 Drucköileitungen
für Arbeitszylinder
3 Arbeitszylinder
4 Stoßstange für
Spornklappe
5 Lenker für Spornklappe
6 KPZ-Federbein
7 Schmutzfänger
8 Spornrad 560 x 200
9 Radgabel
10 Schäkel
12 Federbeinhebel
13 Durchflußsperre
14 Druckölleitung für
Durchflußsperre
15 Spornrückführung
16 Spornklappe

E 54   Verriegelungsschalter Sporn ausgefahren
E 55   Verriegelungsschalter Sporn eingefahren
E 56 } Kupplungstück für Verriegelungsschalter
E 52 }
E 502 Endschalter Sporn ausgefahren
E 520 Endschalter Sporn eingefahren

Flugzeugbein

1 Zweikantbolzen
2 Schwenkhebel
3 Schwenkstoßstange
4 Gabellagerung
5 Rahmenanschlußkopf
6 Knickstrebe unten
7 Zweikantbolzen
8 Öl-Luftfederbein
9 Schutzhose
10 Innerer Bremsflansch
11 Bremsleitungskupplung
12 Achsknotenstück
13 Lenker
14 Bremsleitung
15 Abschleppschäkel
16 Federbeinrahmen
17 Bremsleitung-Trennstelle
18 Ölauffang mit Leitung

Ausbau des Laufrades

1 Lenker   6 Laufrad
2 Achsknotenstück   7 Äußeres Bremsschild
3 Innerer Bremsflansch 8 Äußerer Bremsflansch
4 Laufradachse   9 Trennstelle
5 Leitungskupplung   10 Sechskantbolzen

Fahrgestellhälfte, links

1 Arbeitszylinder für Verkleidungsklappe hinten
2 Lagerung der Knickstrebe oben
3 Verkleidungsklappe hinten
4 Stoßstange für Verkleidungsklappe vorn
5 Verkleidungsklappe vorn
6 Knickstrebe unten
7 Öl-Luftfederbein
8 Ledermanschette
9 Laufrad
10 Federbeinrahmen
11 Schwenkhebel
12 Lagerung des Federbeinrahmens
13 Schwenkstoßstange
14 Knickstrebe oben
15 Arbeitszylinder für
Fahrgestellhälfte

Sturzflugbremsklappe mit Betätigungsteil (linker Tragflügel)

1 Stoßstange
2 Hebel
3 Anzeigevorrichtung
4 Hebelwelle
5 Hebelwellen-Mittelstück
6 Verriegelungsgehäuse
7 Gehäuse des Betätigungsteiles
8 Sturzflugbremsklappe
Hc 25 Verriegelungs-Steuerschieber
Hc 26 Arbeitszylinder

Tragflügel, links
Querruder außen
Querruder innen
Trimmruder
a Ausgleichruder Federsteuerung

5 Landeklappe
6 Ausleger am Endspant
7 Ausleger am Querverband IV
8 Verstellbares Gelenk

Ausleger am Querverband IV und am Endspant

Arado Ar 234B 'Blitz'

Country of origin: Germany.
Type: Single-seat, land-based reconnaissance bomber.
Dimensions: Wing span 47ft 4½in *14.44m*; length 41ft 7½in *12.69m*; height 13ft 8½in *4.18m*; wing area 298 sq ft *27.68m²*.
Weights: Empty 11,466kg *5200kg*;

normal loaded 18,544lb *8410kg*; maximum 21,719lb *9850kg*.
Powerplant: Two Junkers Jumo 004B axial-flow turbojets each of 1985lb *900kg* static thrust.
Performance: Maximum speed 466mph *750kph* at 19,700ft *6000m*; time to 19,700ft, 17.5min; service ceiling 37,730ft

11,500m; range (clean) 1012 miles *1630km*.
Armament: Up to 3305lb *1500kg* of bombs on fuselage and nacelle racks, plus two fixed 20mm MG 151 cannon.
Service: First flight (Ar 234 V1) 15 June 1943, (B-0) 8 June 1944; service entry (B-1) September 1944.

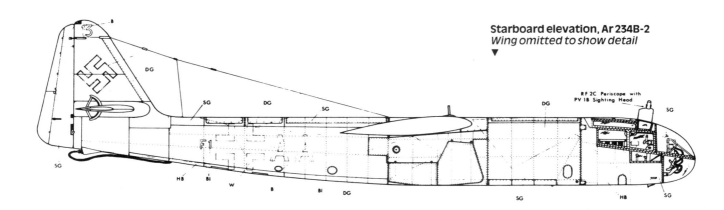

Starboard elevation, Ar 234B-2
Wing omitted to show detail
▼

▲
The Ar 234 was the world's first jet bomber, but it saw limited service. This B-2 was one of several examples acquired by the British at the close of hostilities.

Fuselage cross-sections
▼

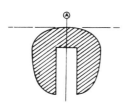
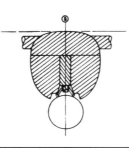
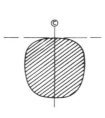
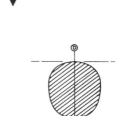
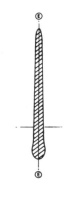

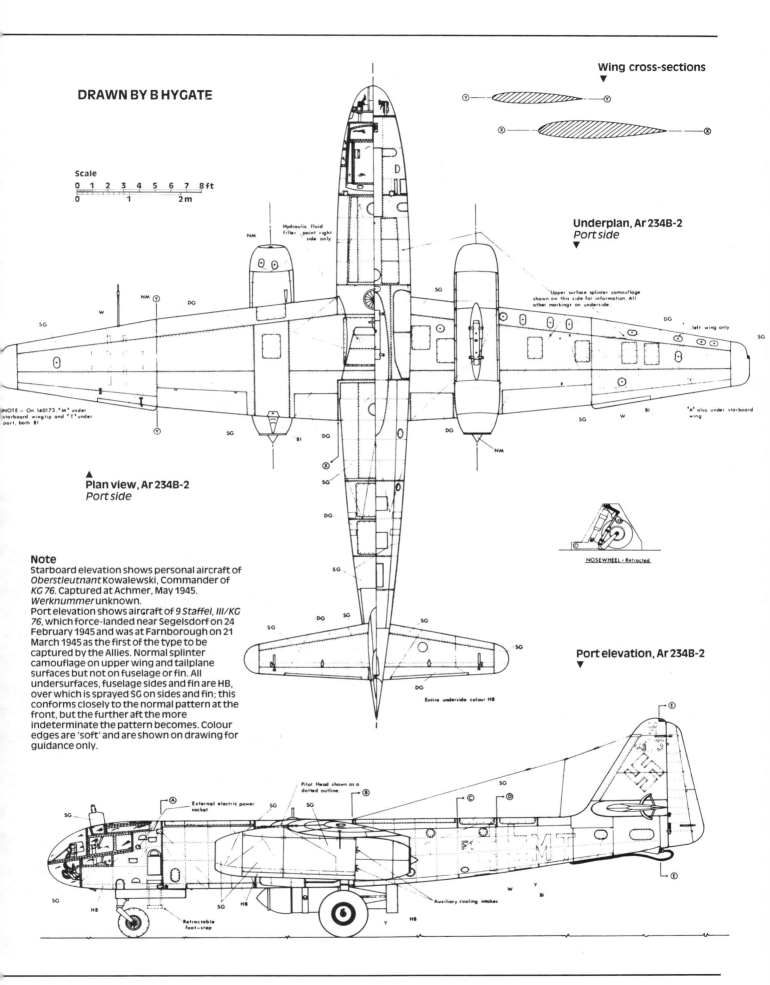

DRAWN BY B HYGATE

Wing cross-sections ▼

Scale
0 1 2 3 4 5 6 7 8 ft
0 1 2 m

Hydraulic fluid filler point right side only

Underplan, Ar 234B-2
Port side ▼

Upper surface splinter camouflage shown on this side for information. All other markings on underside.

left wing only

'A' also under starboard wing

NOTE:- On 140173, 'M' under starboard wingtip and 'T' under port, both Bl

▲
Plan view, Ar 234B-2
Port side

NOSEWHEEL – Retracted

Note
Starboard elevation shows personal aircraft of *Oberstleutnant* Kowalewski, Commander of *KG 76*. Captured at Achmer, May 1945. *Werknummer* unknown.
Port elevation shows aircraft of *9 Staffel, III/KG 76*, which force-landed near Segelsdorf on 24 February 1945 and was at Farnborough on 21 March 1945 as the first of the type to be captured by the Allies. Normal splinter camouflage on upper wing and tailplane surfaces but not on fuselage or fin. All undersurfaces, fuselage sides and fin are HB, over which is sprayed SG on sides and fin; this conforms closely to the normal pattern at the front, but the further aft the more indeterminate the pattern becomes. Colour edges are 'soft' and are shown on drawing for guidance only.

Entire underside colour HB

Port elevation, Ar 234B-2 ▼

Pitot Head shown as a dotted outline.

External electric power socket

Retractable foot-step

Auxiliary cooling intakes

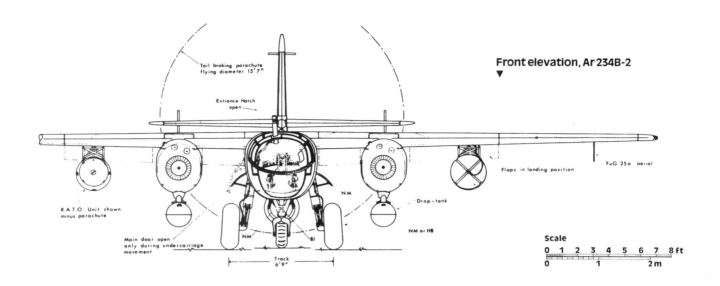

Front elevation, Ar 234B-2
▼

Tail braking parachute
flying diameter 15'7"

Entrance Hatch
open

R.A.T.O. Unit shown
minus parachute

Main door open
only during undercarriage
movement

Track
6'9"

NM

Drop-tank

NM or HB

Flaps in landing position

FuG 25a aerial

BI

Scale

0 1 2 3 4 5 6 7 8 ft

0 1 2m

Scrap port elevation
Engine nacelle (starboard unit)
▼

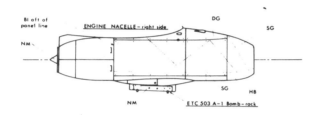

BI aft of
panel line

NM

DG

SG

ENGINE NACELLE – right side

SG HB

NM

ETC 503 A-1 Bomb-rack

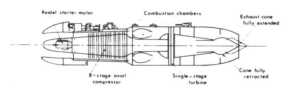

Reidel starter motor

Combustion chambers

Exhaust cone
fully extended

8-stage axial
compressor

Single-stage
turbine

Cone fully
retracted

▲ **Scrap view**
Jumo 109 004B-1 engine

Scrap views
Walter HKW 109-500A-1 RATO unit
▼

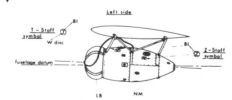

Left side

T-Stoff
symbol
W disc

BI

BI

Z-Stoff
symbol

fuselage datum

LB

NM

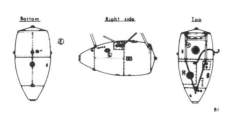

Bottom

Right side

Top

BI

Colour code

SG – *Schwarzgrün 70* (black-green); **DG** – *Dunkelgrün 71* (dark green); **HB** – *Hellblau 65* (light blue); **NM** – Natural metal; **Bl** – Black; **W** – White; **B** – Blue; **Y** – Yellow; **R** – Red; **G** – *RLM Grau 02* (greenish grey); **LB** – Light brown.

Port inboard profile, Ar 234B-2
▼

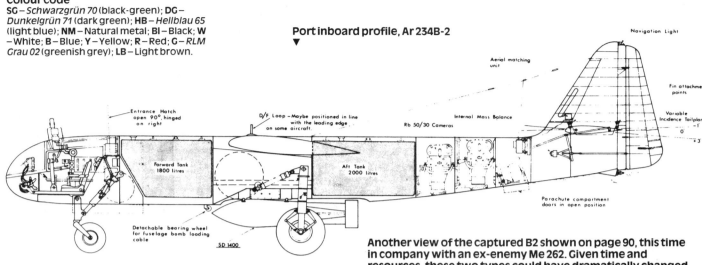

Navigation Light

Aerial matching unit

Fin attachment points

Internal Mass Balance

Rb 50/30 Cameras

Variable Incidence Tailplane

Entrance Hatch open 90°, hinged on right

D/F Loop – Maybe positioned in line with the leading edge on some aircraft.

Forward Tank 1800 litres

Aft Tank 2000 litres

Parachute compartment doors in open position

Detachable bearing wheel for fuselage bomb loading cable

SD 1400

Another view of the captured B2 shown on page 90, this time in company with an ex-enemy Me 262. Given time and resources, these two types could have dramatically changed the outcome of World War II.
▼

VK877

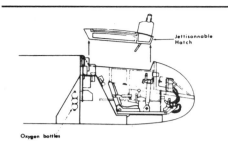

Jettisonnable Hatch

Oxygen bottles

LOTFE 7K
Tachometric Bombsight

Control column

Cockpit interior colour – G

Rear Bulkhead

Instrument panel position

▲
Scrap views
Cockpit details

Numerical key

1. Navigation equipment stowage. 2. Contact altimeter. 3. Nozzle control override switch. 4. Outside air temperature gauge. 5. Height corrector, BZA 1 bomb sight computer. 6. Wind corrector, BZA 1. 7. Rectified airspeed corrector, BZA 1. 8. Map case. 9. Exhaust nozzle control switch. 10. Cockpit lights rheostat. 11. RATO jettison button and selector panel. 12. Fuel cocks. 13. Auxiliary fuel tank selector switch. 14. Rudder trim wheel and indicator. 15. Ignition switch and warning indicator. 16. Throttle friction damper. 17. Spirit level. 18. Floodlight switches. 19. Throttle quadrant. 20. Emergency master electrics circuit breaker. 21. Hydraulic pressure gauge. 22. Gyro monitor switch. 23. Autopilot channel selectors, elevator/aileron/rudder. 24. Target approach switch. 25. Flap and undercarriage selector panel. 26. Flap and undercarriage position lights. 27. Braking parachute streaming handle. 28. Incidence indicator. 29. Repeater gyro horizon. 30. Autopilot master switch. 31. Braking parachute jettison handle. 32. Opening direct-

vision panel. 33. Standby magnetic compass. 34. Port and starboard EPR gauges. 35. Bomb release button on left control column 'horn'. 36. Pilot heater indicator. 37. Clock. 38. Master compass indicator. 39. Gyro horizon and slip indicator. 40. Rate of climb and descent indicator. 41. Turn control for autopilot (Fast and Slow rate). 42. RF 2C periscopic bomb/gun sight. 43. AFN 2 homing indicator. 44. Port and starboard RPM gauges. 45. Control column (releases forward for use of Lofte 7K bomb sight). 46. Canopy jettison handle. 47. Oxygen hose. 48. Port and starboard fuel pressure gauges. 49. Bomb jettison handle. 50. Flare pistol mounting. 51. Oil pressure gauges. 52. Fire warning temperature gauges. 53. Oxygen regulator. 54. Riedel starter motor panel, with RPM gauge high/low range selector buttons. 55. Exhaust gas temperature gauges. 56. Fuel contents gauges (main fuselage tanks only) with Low Fuel Contents lights mounted behind. 57. Oxygen system pressure gauge. 58. Low Fuel Contents indicators. 59. Oxygen flow indicator. 60. Oxygen system on/off cock.

61. Bomb fusing selector panel. 62. Main electrical switch panel. 63. Voltmeters. 64. Bomb sequence selector panel. 65. Navigation lights switch. 66. Frequency selector. 67. FuG 125 – Hermine (bearings from ground rotating beacon). 68. Camera doors operating handle. 69. FuG 25A IFF. 70. Camera operating panel. 71. FuG 25A demolition switch. 72. Flap and undercarriage emergency selector. 73. FuG 16 ZY junction box. 74. Remote control panel for FuG 16ZY homing aerial. 75. Hydraulic hand pump (operates service selected on 72). 76. Control column release knob. 77. Shoulder strap attachment. 78. Mounting for Lofte 7K tachometric bomb sight. 79. Pilot's seat. 80. Cabin conditioning selector. 81. Tailplane trim actuator handle and position indicator. 82. Altitude compensated airspeed indicator. 83. Fine/coarse altimeter. 84. Clock illumination button. 85. R/T transmitter button. 86. Footbrake motors. 87. Ultraviolet cockpit light. 88. Gyro horizon erection switch.

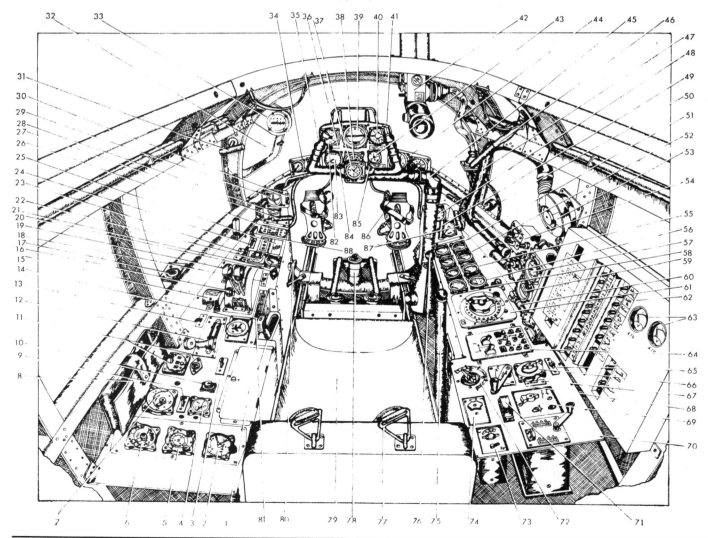

Scrap views
Fuselage- and engine-mounted bomb loading
▼ ▶

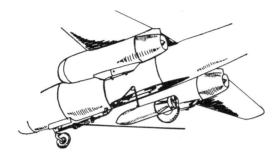

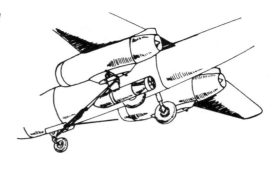

NOTE:– Views below are diagrammatic to show correct shape of tail fins. When fitted to the body, the bomb's tail-cone should be rotated 45° to form an "X". Those shown in aircraft side views are correct. This also applies to AB 250 and 500 bomb-cluster containers. (See sketch.)

Bombs usually coloured HB or NM, but the 500 and 250 kg. bombs may be painted SG, but they still carry the identification stripes.

HB

R

True Lug/Fin Relationship

Bomb Identification Stripes

SC – Yellow
SD – Red   } On tail-cone between
PC – Blue   each set of fins.

300 litre DROP-TANK

Scrap views ▶
Typical weapons

| PC 1400 'Fritz' | SC 1000 'Hermann' | SD 1000 'Esau' | PC 500 RS | SC 500J | SD 500 | SC 250 | SD 250 | AB 250 | AB 500 |

fusing connection

suspension lug

Maximum normal load :–1000 kgs.
Maximum overload with R.A.T.O.:–1500 kgs.
Maximum load under each nacelle :–500 kgs.

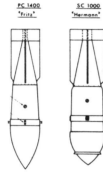

Scrap view
Walter 109-500A-1 RATO unit (rear part of nacelle removed)

Scrap view
Lofte 7K tachometric bomb sight
▼

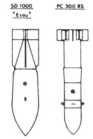

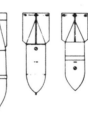

Scrap view
Nose gear layout
▲

◀ **Scrap view**
Reconnaissance camera controls

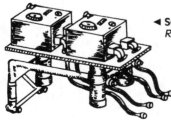

Scrap view ▶
Main undercarriage, port side

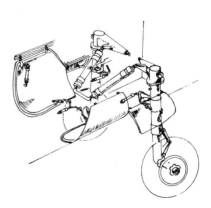

The Publisher wishes to thank the
following draughtsmen whose drawings
appear in this volume

J D CARRICK   BJÖRN KARLSTRÖM
D H COOKSEY   PAT LLOYD
PETER G COOKSLEY   J D McHARD
GEORGE COX   K A MERRICK
GEOFF DUVAL   IAN R STAIR
B HYGATE   J WENSTEDT
HARRY WOODMAN